I thought I had written the last chapter in tragedy when our son, Jimmy, died of leukaemia at the age of eight. I was wrong. Sue Grant's moving account of Alex's illness and death seared through my soul afresh; her words transported me back to the role of helpless observer, unable to prevent the suffering and death of yet another young life. What could be crueller than the irony of a body wrecked by the treachery of its own malfunctioning cells? What indeed – except Alex himself, as he started out on life with all the optimism, sensitivity and dignity of new adulthood, only to be suddenly enslaved to a painful existence of total dependence. Alex's story was one for which cancer itself had already written the last chapter. However, his mother's beautiful book is a postscript to cancer, proof that not even cancer can destroy Alex's spirit, as he walks ahead of us leading the way on his two blue sticks, an indestructible symbol of courage and love. Shame on us humans, who invent ever better ways to kill each other instead of pooling human resources worldwide to find the cure and prevention of cancer. But we won't give up, Alex. We won't.

Jane Renouf, journalist and author of
Jimmy – No Time to Die, *HarperCollins*

When I started to read *Standing On His Own Two Feet,* interruptions became a source of real resentment – I just wanted to read and read to the end. Sue Grant not only has a real-life tragedy to tell, but she tells it with such lucidity and artistry that the reader is drawn into the story effortlessly.

I found myself entering into the experiences and emotions she describes, the more so because of her honesty, sensitivity and occasional humour and a refreshing absence of sentimentality. This is not only a book from which health care professionals could gain invaluable insights, but one which has the potential to make any reader more fully human.

Sister Frances Dominica, founder of Helen House Children's Hospice,
Oxford, and Douglas House, a respice for young adults, Oxford

D1319254

of related interest

Attending to the Fact - Staying with Dying
Hilary Elfick and David Head
Foreword by Andrew Hoy
ISBN 1 84310 247 1

Being Mindful, Easing Suffering
Reflections on Palliative Care
Christopher Johns
ISBN 1 84310 212 9

Spirituality, Healing and Medicine
Return to the Silence
David Aldridge
ISBN 1 85302 554 2

Writing My Way Through Cancer
Myra Schneider
ISBN 1 84310 113 0

Health, the Individual, and Integrated Medicine
Revisiting an Aesthetic of Health Care
David Aldridge
ISBN 1 84310 232 3

Journeys into Palliative Care
Roots and Reflections
Edited by Christina Mason
ISBN 1 84310 030 4

Spirituality in Health Care Contexts
Edited by Helen Orchard
Foreword by Julia Neuberger
ISBN 1 85302 969 6

Standing On His Own Two Feet

A Diary of Dying

Sue Grant

Foreword by David Clark

Jessica Kingsley Publishers
London and Philadelphia

All rights reserved. No part of this publication may be reproduced in any material form (including photocopying or storing it in any medium by electronic means and whether or not transiently or incidentally to some other use of this publication) without the written permission of the copyright owner except in accordance with the provisions of the Copyright, Designs and Patents Act 1988 or under the terms of a licence issued by the Copyright Licensing Agency Ltd, 90 Tottenham Court Road, London, England W1T 4LP. Applications for the copyright owner's written permission to reproduce any part of this publication should be addressed to the publisher.

Warning: The doing of an unauthorised act in relation to a copyright work may result in both a civil claim for damages and criminal prosecution.

The right of Sue Grant to be identified as author of this work has been asserted by her in accordance with the Copyright, Designs and Patents Act 1988.

This edition first published in 2005
by Jessica Kingsley Publishers
116 Pentonville Road
London N1 9JB, UK
and
400 Market Street, Suite 400
Philadelphia, PA 19106, USA

www.jkp.com

Copyright © Sue Grant 2005
Foreword copyright © David Clark 2005

Library of Congress Cataloging in Publication Data

Grant, Sue, 1954-
   Standing on his own two feet : a diary of dying / Sue Grant ; Foreword by David Clark.
      p. cm.
   ISBN-13: 978-1-84310-368-4 (pbk.)
   ISBN-10: 1-84310-368-0 (pbk.)
   1. Grant, Alexander--Health. 2. Bones--Cancer--Patients--Great Britain--Biography. 3. Terminally ill--Great Britain--Biography. I. Title.
   RC280.B6G735 2005
   362.196'99471'0092--dc22

2005001867

British Library Cataloguing in Publication Data
A CIP catalogue record for this book is available from the British Library

ISBN-13: 978 1 84310 368 4
ISBN-10: 1 84310 368 0

Printed and Bound in Great Britain by
Athenaeum Press, Gateshead, Tyne and Wear

For Alexander with Love

Contents

Foreword

In the rich world, we have become used to making assumptions about our health and the health of our children. We make plans for the future, expect to live a long life and dream idly of what we will do when our working days are over. Unless our personal experience teaches us otherwise, we do not ponder much on the possibility of a life cut short. This book reminds us of the fragility of such assumptions. It takes us into a world where illness and disease conspire to shorten and take away life and in so doing turn upside down the worlds of those involved.

Alexander had just begun studies at Warwick University, and was settling to life in England after a childhood spent mainly in Germany. Before Christmas in the first semester he developed a problem with his knee that saw him returning home in December looking pale, emaciated and in increasing pain. He was diagnosed with osteosarcoma, a rare and aggressive bone cancer.

This book is Alexander's story, as told by his mother. No one will find it easy to read. It is a book that wrenches at the heart and churns the stomach. Its narrative is at times almost too painful to follow. It may well anger and frustrate those who read it. Yet it is a story that had to be told and from which we can receive and learn beyond measure. I have no doubt that I am the better for having read it.

Sue Grant describes a world darkly alien to many, and yet wearyingly familiar to those who have been there. Her book centres around the trajectory of Alexander's illness and associated treatment. Along the way we gain insights into the health care systems of both Germany and Britain. We see how, at their best, such systems can provide uniquely personal care tailored precisely to the needs of patients and families. We also see how often that goal can remain unrealized, ignored even, as the medical-bureaucratic juggernaut gathers speed and the goals of treatment and care fail to be properly examined.

Above all, Sue Grant teaches us something about families and their resilience, even against tremendous odds. She shows how such resilience shines through in the midst of Alexander's illness. We learn how it is maintained among the ongoing routines of the family, the demanding lives of other adolescent siblings, the pressures of work, money, and maintaining some sense of daily routine. It is a story of devastating illness, but also of meals, shopping, family treats and rituals.

Standing On His Own Two Feet will no doubt be read by parents who have had similar experiences. Certainly it should be read by health and social care professionals working in oncology and with those who are dying. Pastors, priests, teachers, counsellors and many others will find that it has something to offer them as they go about their work. Ultimately though, this is a book for anyone to read. It is about the premature death of a remarkable young man who faced up to the terrible demands of his treatment, who came to terms with his disability and who, in time, gazed on the fact of his own mortality with a wisdom beyond his years.

Ultimately, this is a book about life and its many imperfections. We are privileged indeed that Sue Grant has felt able to write it.

David Clark
Professor of Medical Sociology
University of Lancaster, UK

Prologue

'Don't do it,' said a doctor-friend when I told her I wanted to bring my terminally ill son home. I'd no idea how exhausting and emotionally draining this caring business is, she warned. Honestly, I'd be much better off leaving him in hospital till the end, and anyway I should think of myself and the rest of the family. They need a mother too.

So I thought of myself, my son and the rest of the family. And I brought him home. There wasn't much more to consider. That he wouldn't have to die in hospital was a promise we made him when he was first diagnosed with cancer. Only then we didn't – *couldn't* – believe it would actually happen to our child.

The first encounter with death on the ward opened my eyes. Two nurses were pushing a bed – its human occupant covered with a white sheet – towards the lift. One was fighting to keep back the tears. The other opted for a life-goes-on attitude.

No sooner had the lift shaft swallowed them up than the cleaner stormed into the empty room. Personal possessions found their way into a black, plastic bin liner, marked with a sticky label for the relatives. The still-perky daffodils in the uniform hospital vase stood no chance. They had to take leave of life just like their former owner and disappeared head first into a blue rubbish sack. With a single, nonchalant move of her arm, a nurse wiped out the name of the deceased on the station's wall chart. An hour later, the next doomed patient moved into the room, which reeked of disinfectant.

My son should fare better. Not even the well-meant offer of a chic two-bed room with all mod cons could make me change my mind.

True, the cellar door refused to shut properly. That was because of the tube. From a ventilator resembling a futuristic vacuum cleaner, it snaked its way up the stairs, through the living room door, along the wall, behind the back of the rented hospital bed and up to the oxygen mask on my son's face. If you want to breathe, you need air. But the mechanical production of air was ear-splitting. Which is why the appliance was banned to the basement.

Of course he would have felt happier lying in his own bedroom upstairs. He yearned for privacy and peace, the right to decide what should happen to him (or rather, what should *not* happen to him). But the tiny children's bedroom in our terraced house had not been designed with an intensive care unit in mind.

We compromised by agreeing to adapt the living room so that it would suit the requirements of the bed-ridden patient, but also leave enough space for both medical equipment and family life.

The bulky hospital bed we positioned comfortably in a corner. At the foot end, a small engine purred continuously as it pumped and deflated the pockets of the air mattress. The infusion stand was at the other end. It dispensed litres of saline solution and glucose, day in, day out. Over the bed hung the innocent-looking morphine pump. Non-stop, 24 hours a day, it worked to alleviate the otherwise excruciating pain of bone cancer.

But next to this forest of machines we put our sofa and our chairs. Everywhere within sight of the bed were floral greetings from our friends, and even from his enforced horizontal position, my son could look out of the window and see the sun, the snow-capped trees in the garden and watch the blackbirds searching for food.

The hospital supplied a home care nurse. He brought daily supplies to replace the used infusion bottles, ordered more oxygen, fetched the medicine from the chemist's and, most importantly, monitored the morphine pump. Everything else we did ourselves.

The technical challenges were overcome. But how do you feel as you wait for your child to die?

The last five weeks were long. Five weeks, when every hour, every minute, becomes precious. My son's unwavering decision to refuse any further attempts at treatment was difficult to accept in the beginning. Maybe something could still lead to a last minute miracle? Perhaps he could still win just a little more time on earth? He was more realistic than us. He was right and we learnt to take our cue from him.

Once we were free of the hospital, the tension and pressure began to fall away. Even I now understood that there would be no miracle. That any treatment would have been both useless and inhuman. That he was going to die. And that he wanted to go – and could go.

Because I could not make him well again I felt helpless. But being able to support him in his wish to die in the familiarity of his own home with his family around him was a great consolation.

The last days were suddenly free of fear. Time was incredibly valuable. All the crushing worries, torments and pain of the preceding months simply floated away. They no longer touched us. Our daily routine relaxed. He didn't want the dressing on his thin arm changed today? Fine. Let's do it tomorrow. Or not at all. It didn't matter any more.

Instead we had lots of time to exchange memories, to be close together, undisturbed by the noise and inevitable hectic environment of a hospital ward. The metastases in his lungs made speaking difficult. Eating and drinking were things of the past. Yet we felt good. We treated ourselves to one last picnic: me with a cheese roll and he with a fresh bottle of glucose. We laughed with delight.

During the last nights I slept next to him on the floor on a mattress. Until then, he had wished to be alone. Now that he was too weak to operate his bed's remote control, he was afraid of being on his own in the dark.

Both of us – mother and father – camped on the living room floor that final night. His brother and sister waited upstairs. So when the end came, we could hardly have asked for a more beautiful one. We were all with him and could let him go peacefully, gently and with great dignity.

Am I glad that I did it.

1

Starting Out

A lexander never tired of hearing the story of how he had spent his foetal months in Scotland, listening in to his student mother's lectures on German literature at Edinburgh University, soaking up early linguistic skills in the translation classes and supplying the odd physical impetus during the final exams.

Only a couple of litres of water and some overstretched skin separated Alexander from receiving a degree in person. As it was, I accepted the scroll for both of us and then rejoined my husband Wolfgang at our student digs in Bavaria. Two months later he drove me to the clinic as soon as the first contractions came, just as the doctor had instructed. But the midwife was singularly unimpressed by my nocturnal efforts and, muttering remarks to the tune of 'inexperienced young mothers' and 'this will take hours yet', sent Wolfgang back home and tucked me into bed along with a number of machines before settling down somewhere out of sight to try and snatch some sleep herself.

That was when I realized that my knowledge of German was selective. I would have had no difficulty in discussing the finer points of Baroque lyrics or even current federal economic policy, but I was at a complete loss for the right words to attract the attention of a nameless, invisible and somewhat grumpy midwife in the dark of the night. By the time I had worked out a halfway acceptable formula and then convinced her that my baby was going to be born *now*, I was too exhausted to do much more about it. So it was fortunate that she remembered to call Wolfgang just in time.

Nobody had told me what forceps can do to a baby's head. In fact, I hadn't even realized that a team of doctors had shoehorned my firstborn into the world. What with his shock of black hair spread unevenly over his strangely elongated skull, Alexander would not have won a beauty competition, at least for the first three days.

But of course it didn't matter. He was our baby boy and we loved him just as he was. It was 17 September and I was twenty-two.

A week after leaving hospital, we moved out of our student digs and into adult life. Although both Wolfgang and I are born and bred townies, we dreamed of raising a family in a country cottage barely visible behind a hedge of hollyhocks, a few sheep grazing in the backyard and everyone thriving on home-grown organic food. Finding a small, rented flat high on an inaccessible hill, tucked away behind the city, satisfied our craving for a back-to-nature style of living, surrounded as we were by peaceful countryside and family smallholdings.

We invested somewhat reluctantly in a second hand car so that Wolfgang could reach the outlying village schools where he now worked as a trainee teacher. Whilst he struggled to find his feet, paint the flat and take on a father's role, I settled down to the unfamiliar business of being a foreigner, a housewife and a mother to an inquisitive, now blond and curly-headed Alexander.

Right from the outset, he surprised us with his headstrong character, burning desire to discover and understand the world around him, intense perseverance and commitment to matters he cared about, but also his shyness and often moody aloofness.

As though he knew instinctively that he wouldn't have much time to waste, he concentrated on the important parts of life, producing his first tooth at three months, gulping his food down as fast as possible even though he was then racked with hiccups, examining the wheels on his cot and not wasting valuable minutes with maternal cuddles and kisses. He had no patience with crawling either. Why bother when you can walk and run at ten months?

Four weeks later, while we were on holiday in England, our bundle of energy suddenly crumpled up with stomach pains and diarrhoea. We rushed him to the doctor who tested him for suspected salmonella and late that night a phone call came through, telling us to take Alexander straight to the hospital first thing in the morning. It looked serious, we were warned. All night, Wolfgang held his baby son as he writhed, tormented by waves of cramps. We tried not to dwell too much on the bleak medical prognosis.

Next morning we presented ourselves dutifully at the hospital where we then had to wait. Alexander seemed to be in no discomfort and amused himself by running at breakneck speed up and down the extremely long corridor. Eventually a doctor appeared, peered at the assorted collection of waiting patients and asked where that desperately ill baby with salmonella was. He was not the only one to look mystified as we scooped up an annoyed Alexander just as he was completing another lap.

Much to our relief, it turned out that it was a less virulent strain. The shadow of imminent death dissolved as quickly as it had appeared.

Another challenge, but of a more agreeable nature, was language. Our son might have been living physically in Germany, but we were determined to pass on, to the best of our ability, a love for both of our own mother tongues and respective cultures. Bearing in mind what I had learned about bilingualism at university, we devised a system whereby I would play the English-speaking anchor, and Wolfgang the German.

In the long run, this system served all our children well. But with Alexander the scales tipped heavily on the English side at the beginning, perhaps as a result of his being exposed more to English than German, or perhaps because he simply had a predilection for the English phoneme.

At two-and-a-half he was a proficient English speaker with only a rudimentary grasp of German, a fact that became clear to us very suddenly one day when we lost him. We were visiting Alexander's grandparents in Munich and Wolfgang was busy in their garden fitting out our latest vehicle as a camping bus. Alexander found the whole business exciting – so exciting that he would ask his dad when our roving tent on wheels would be ready for use, then run a circuit through the garden and round the house and hope to find the job completed on his return. When it wasn't, he simply repeated the question and the marathon.

It took Wolfgang a while to realize that Alexander had disappeared. The whole family searched everywhere for him, to no avail. After 20 minutes, we were so concerned that we phoned the police and reported our small son missing. We gave a description of his clothes, height, colour of his hair and then remembered to say that he spoke English and little German.

When they found him, unharmed and unperturbed, and still running at a cracking pace an hour later and 3 km away, the police had had enough time to brush up their English. In answer to their questions, he told them that he was looking for a shop that sold bus potties, because his father didn't seem to have put one into our camping van and he thought we might need one as it was an awful long way to England. It was hard to say who was more impressed – the police or Alexander – as he clambered out of the police car that brought him home.

Our daughter Natalie was born two years after her older brother, and two days after Alexander's fourth birthday Benjamin completed our growing family. The two-bedroom flat suffered from acute congestion. My love affair with country life had quickly fizzled out once I realized I was staring at fields of chemically sprayed strawberries and the last moments of the landlord's rabbits as they awaited execution outside our bedroom window. Because the bus service ran only twice a day and three small children had to be negotiated in and out of doors, I spent most of the time isolated on top of the hill, with few opportunities to meet people and make friends. I felt lonely and homesick.

So we decided to abandon country life and move back to the hub of the city. The Golden Cross is a massive stone building dating back to the fourteenth century and was once the medieval Hilton to all passing royalty and celebrities. With its castellated roof, solid Gothic entrance gates sealing the quiet inner courtyard off at night from the general public, and its commanding position at the head of one of Germany's most beautiful squares, it was a literal case of your home is your castle. We gladly accepted an offer to rent a completely refurbished, light and spacious flat on the top floor, overlooking the square at the front and the courtyard at the back.

Four-year-old Alexander could hardly wait to move. Armed with a kettle – his contribution to carrying things – he raced ahead up the stairs (for structural reasons there was no lift) and then stopped in his tracks.

'Mummy, we've forgotten Ben!' he shouted, thoroughly upset to think that we had carelessly left his six-month-old baby brother behind in an empty flat. For a moment, he had me worried. But on second thoughts, I knew without a shade of doubt that the baby was soundly asleep in the carry cot, wedged between pots and pans at the back of the van. Alexander remained unconvinced. I had to go all the way down again with him to where Wolfgang was waiting with Natty and extricate the baby from all the mess before he was reassured.

Sleeping in a new bedroom with a ceiling four metres high was a scary experience. 'Will the trees fall down?' Alexander inquired nervously at the sight of the solid wooden beams with a width of a woman's forearm running through all the rooms. They didn't, but possibly they endangered our lives in a different way. All of them had been freshly coated with a chemical preservative and, years later, the next tenants, worried about recurrent headaches and poor health, called for tests to be carried out. These revealed abnormally high toxic levels. Everything had to be stripped down and cleaned up.

But we were blissfully unaware of the danger lurking above. At last there was enough space inside for the children to run, roll and jump. Walls a metre thick swallowed up the accompanying noise, allowing cordial relationships with the neighbours on the other side and underneath us.

From the living room window we had a regal view of daily life in the street below, something I greatly appreciated whenever the children were ill and we were imprisoned within the castle confines. I would prop the children up on cushions in the ample window sill and they would forget their coughs and runny tummies and chicken pox for a while as we counted passing buses, played 'I spy', or just watched humanity go past.

On one occasion, a high-ranking but controversial German politician held a keynote speech outside in the square. Security was tight. Members of the special riot squad were posted in strategic positions – such as on our roof – to monitor the movements of demonstrators. Alexander and I watched, fascinated, as the armed forces concealed up above carefully walky-talked the ground forces into forming an ever tighter circle around the unsuspecting, banner-waving, whistle-blowing antagonists in the crowd and then simply ejected them from the arena. Since then, I have had no trouble in visualizing the meaning of the medical term 'harnessing free radicals'.

If there was a disadvantage to the new living arrangements, it was the lack of a garden. We compensated by choosing a kindergarten situated in the middle of a nearby park. Once we had rattled Ben's buggy over the cobblestones and manoeuvred the four of us round a few more narrow inner-city pavements, we were suddenly away from the medieval stone and immersed in an oasis of green.

There was, of course, a reason why the kindergarten was so situated. The park had once been a cemetery and the idyllic building, now alive with the sound of laughing children, had served as the mortuary. But we didn't know this until Alexander started digging. A children's television programme explaining the formation of the earth had started him thinking.

Quite logically, he had worked out that Bavaria must be roughly opposite Australia on planet Earth and, to test his hypothesis, he began excavating, convinced that at the end of the tunnel he would find Down Under. Such was his enthusiasm for this mammoth project that he succeeded in organizing a nursery chain gang. For two days running, the three-year-olds trudged backwards and forwards with sand buckets, while the six-year-olds bent double at the spades. But although a number of bones came to the surface, Australia didn't, and one by one the others lost interest and disappeared in search of less exerting distractions.

Alexander did not give up. His teacher checked up on him every now and again, a solitary figure still flinging clods of earth out of the gaping hole. Another back-breaking week passed before he finally ran out of steam, still sure that Australia was there somewhere, if only he could have dug further.

The nursery school years were also the picnic years. On fine days in summer we would meet at lunchtime to devour the packed lunch I brought along. All we had to do was walk a few yards away from the kindergarten building, spread out the rug on our favourite spot in the shade of an ancient plane tree and tuck in to the egg mayonnaise sandwiches. Sometimes Wolfgang was able to join us later, so we waited for him, passing the time by watching the ants on the bark of the tree. More often than not he would find the children lying on their backs, knees in the air, listening quietly to a special 'picnic story'. Afterwards we would drift off to the adventure playground in another corner of the park before making our way home late in the afternoon, tired and grubby, but usually happy.

Once Ben had turned three and was elevated to kindergarten child status, I felt it was high time to start building a career. I had gladly stayed at home for seven years to look after the children while they were very small, but now I needed something for myself. Much to my delight, I quickly found part-time work as a teacher of English for a large company and, before long, more courses in the local adult education centre.

Working in the morning while the family was out, or in the evenings when Wolfgang was at home, turned out to be a practical arrangement that we all profited from.

Received wisdom maintained that the beginning of school life would signal the end of our children's bilingualism. As their German environ-ment grew in importance, so the argument went, they would be less and less inclined to play odd man out and speak English. At least in public. Even though I found this theory hard to swallow, I will admit to feeling somewhat apprehensive when slim, fair-haired Alexander became a schoolboy, three days before his sixth birthday and as the youngest in his class.

During the initial phase of adapting to the new situation, most mothers trundled along to school with toddlers and babies in tow, once at 7.45 in the morning to deliver their first-graders, then again at 10.30 to collect them. Great was the excitement on both sides when the children rushed down the steps, brandishing paintings and trailing school satchels, to the immense pride of the waiting mothers.

One day, Alexander was so effervescent about his morning at school that he shouted down to me while still on the steps – loud and clear for all to hear, and in English.

Two bigger, tough-looking lads turned round to stare. Alexander was quite oblivious, still gabbling away innocently in English about his deeds. The boys walked over, hands in pockets and a nasty jeer on their faces.

'Why don't you talk German?' they asked accusingly. 'You must be one of them foreigners,' they added menacingly.

There was nothing I could do. Instinct told me that Alexander's response to this situation would determine whether English remained on the menu. Suddenly he seemed so very fragile and vulnerable, standing there alone.

'I speak two languages, English and German. Can you only speak one?' he retorted with such disarming confidence that the boys were stunned into an embarrassed silence and slouched off. Was I proud of my little son! From that moment on there was never another doubt in my mind that Alexander and Britain were inseparable.

School introduced him to two new factors. Within the school's catchment area was the temporary accommodation for visiting professors and their families from around the world on short-term contracts with the university. In no time, Alexander had befriended the new international infant intake and was off to chopstick parties galore.

Being able to read opened up the second door. The one most frequently used led to the town library, conveniently situated in the building next to our castle, so Alexander could go backwards and forwards safely on his own.

Everything under the sun interested him. He could not borrow enough books fast enough. But even I was taken aback when he returned on one occasion staggering under the weight of two carrier bags, which, on closer inspection, turned out to contain no less than 37 books. Rather stupidly, I asked him whatever he was planning to do with so many books and received the tart reply: 'Read them.' It took him three days and then he went back for more.

Alexander simply loved books. The antics of Pooh Bear with his adult British humour never failed to amuse him. If any of the children were ill, the standard procedure was for me to read a story from Volume 4 of my own much-loved, musty 1930s children's encyclopaedia. This was a special treat and reserved solely for such moments. It nearly always worked.

A day just wasn't complete without a goodnight story, snuggled up on the sofa with his brother and sister as we read our way through the years and the children's classics. At the ripe old age of fourteen, Alexander was still not above dropping in to listen. Nor was the long, tiresome drive from the south of Germany to Calais, the ferry crossing and subsequent search for a bed and breakfast in England an excuse for missing out on the evening ritual.

I still remember one particularly exhausting trip. We had all thankfully plopped into diverse beds in our family room somewhere in Dover and I was hoping nobody would want a story that night. But there was no getting past Alexander.

At the time, I was attempting to read *Tarka the Otter* and finding the language over-ambitious for my young listeners. Normally, I would have rephrased the more difficult words as I was reading out loud, but that night I was too tired to think. As I battled on with the unabridged version, the room went quiet before settling down to a concert of whiffles and snores. I could hardly keep my eyes open and as nobody seemed to be awake any more, let alone listening, I ground to a gentle halt mid-chapter.

Silence for all of two minutes. Then a tousled head appeared from the top bunk. 'And what happened *then?*' inquired Alexander brightly.

A goodnight story and a holiday in Britain came top of Alexander's list of nicest things on earth. How we all looked forward to the annual family expedition. It took days of preparation before we were ready to head north, and as long as the children were small, we went armed with occupational therapy. One of the all-time favourites was the map.

Each child was issued with a pack containing felt tips and a large and severely simplified (because hand-drawn) map of our route. Starting point was our castle, represented by a tower pictogram. This then merged into a sweeping motorway, divided into segments, that cut across roughly defined countries and led straight to a picture of a ship which just fitted into the English Channel. On the other side, our destination would be marked with a triumphant and romantic-looking cottage icon.

The idea was that, as we crawled along the autobahn, the children would then track our progress across Europe by colouring in the appropriate section on the map and, according to age and ability, garnish it with additional extras such as national borders or sheep or squiggles.

Although it was certainly effective in eliminating the dreaded question 'Are we nearly there yet?', the cunning map plan proved to be counterproductive after all. Now all we heard was: 'Mummy, can I colour in the next bit of the map now?'

Standing on deck and watching the white cliffs of Dover float into view was always a thrilling experience, topped perhaps only by the joy of waking up the following morning to the smell of bacon frying and the screeching of seagulls.

Alexander in particular relished this annual reunification and was truly miserable when one year, by way of an experiment, we took the overnight ferry from Zeebrugge to Harwich, depriving ourselves of that magical first morning on home ground. We never did it again.

Over the years we explored the whole of the British Isles. Traditional seaside holidays on the south coast, showing the children the havens of my own childhood memories, a cold and wet holiday in Wales, which the children loved because there was a dead sheep on the beach and the wind howled so nicely past our remote cottage as we read *The Secret Garden* in the evenings, to picking heather in the wide-open expanses of the Scottish Highlands, every holiday filled in a cultural gap.

The children swung cricket bats, ate fish and chips out of the obligatory newspaper, rode upstairs on double-decker buses on the *left-hand* side of the road, watched *Blue Peter* on television, caught mackerel off the Cornish coast, walked out to St Michael's Mount on the causeway and gazed in awe at Robin Hood's tree in Sherwood Forest. We would return home laden with the usual expat survival kit of Marmite, Oxo cubes, digestive biscuits and jelly.

The latter developed cult status. Whereas other families felt obliged to honour the school achievements of their offspring with smart watches, bikes or cash handouts, we managed quite satisfactorily with a celebration jelly. Reward by jelly in our family has a proven track record and we even started importing it for others to try too.

Of course there were occasions when we needed the opposite of raspberry fluff and cream. The odd childish prank, like the time Alexander meticulously filled balloons with water and then dropped them out of our fifth-floor window to watch with malicious glee as they burst on the cobbled courtyard below, showering the freshly coiffured ladies coming out of the hairdresser's, was no reason for despair. Harder to deal with was sibling rivalry. Between Alexander and Natty this remained generally on a verbal level, but the temptation for the older sibling to exert physical force on a brother four years his junior frequently proved too strong.

Poor Ben often had to be rescued from Alexander's steel grip or be given the blow-rub-and-now-it-won't-hurt-any-more treatment after his brother had dragged him across the floor. It seemed a vicious circle: Alexander would invariably be the offender, Ben the victim. If Ben had been born first, the problem would have been reversed.

We tried all the usual parental tricks to defuse such situations, sometimes with success, sometimes not. It was in the aftermath of one of the unsuccessful attempts that tempers ran high all round. An indignant and mortally offended eight-year-old Alexander announced that he was leaving home as he could not live with this terrible family any longer. If he was a trifle surprised to hear me agreeing with him wholeheartedly, he didn't show it. As far as I was concerned, I just needed to know where he intended moving to, I explained, so I could send on his things.

After a little thought, he decided his grandparents would fit the bill. I suggested he gave them a ring to put them in the picture and warn them that he would be arriving with the next train. 'Can't Daddy drive me there?', a slightly anxious-looking Alexander inquired. We thought not. At least, not under the present circumstances. If he wanted to do his own thing, he would have to manage the 90-minute train journey to Munich alone, we said firmly.

Alexander rose to the challenge, phoned his grandparents, packed a suitcase, ignored his goggle-eyed brother and sister and demanded to be taken to the railway station, *please*.

All of us went with him, a defiant, hurting little boy who was not going to back down now. We helped him choose a carriage, handed him his ticket – a single – had a quiet word with the ticket collector behind his back, then stood on the platform, waving cordially to the top of his blond head, feeling more worried than we dared admit at letting him travel alone for the first time and secretly full of admiration for his courage.

His phone call the next day can only be described as condescending. Life was much more pleasant in his new surroundings, he said. Grandma made him apple cake every day and nobody ever scolded. It was heavenly. He had no plans for coming back.

By the time he rang again, four days later, the frayed tempers had softened. His voice sounded small as he confessed that his grandparents made him go to bed much too early and he had read all the books there, so it wasn't very nice any more and he was coming back home. Please come to meet him at the station. What a heart-warming home coming we had, all the quarrels forgotten and glad to have our headstrong son safely back with us again!

His steadfastness greatly impressed Natty, who decided that if her big brother could go to Munich on his own, she could certainly manage to fly to England all by herself and visit her English grandma. A couple of weeks later, we all drove to the airport to deliver our six-year-old daughter into the capable hands of the stewardess for the duration of the 90-minute flight to Heathrow. She had a wonderful three-week holiday there and Ben would certainly have followed suit too, if my mother had not died of cancer a year later.

Our days spent in our castle were, however, numbered. After the cramped little flat on the hill, this open-plan accommodation had seemed incredibly large. Now we realized it wasn't. At least, not if you want each child to have its own bedroom and your teacher-husband quite rightly needs a study to work in after school finishes at lunchtime. And anyway, we still hadn't quite given up hoping that at some time in the future we would be in a position to buy our own house with a garden.

That chance came out of the blue when friends alerted us to the sale of a medium-sized 50s terrace with a good-sized suburban garden just on the edge of the historic city centre. It needed a complete renovation and a loft conversion, and was situated unpleasantly close to the motorway that sliced its way through an otherwise sought-after residential area, but the price matched our meagre savings, so we took the plunge.

We were high on anticipation and nostalgia at our last Christmas in the castle. For the last time, Wolfgang came home with a tree of a size no doubt designed to grace one of the numerous churches in the city. As usual, we celebrated the British way – with stockings hung up on Christmas Eve for Santa, presents and traditional lunch on 25 December. To even out the balance, we always had a German Easter breakfast in the flat complete with hand-painted eggs hidden behind vases, concealed in the heels of slippers or down the back of the sofa for the children to hunt out on Easter Sunday.

Until they were older, the children had naturally assumed that their German friends did the same things at the same time at Christmas. It came as quite a shock to them when they discovered that their contemporaries opened their presents on Christmas Eve and a heated debate ensued as to whether they, Alexander, Natty and Ben, were not at a severe disadvantage with the English system. In the end, we put it to the vote. They could choose the custom they thought best. But when they realized that a traditional German Christmas does not entail stockings on the 24th, they soon arrived at an unanimous decision to leave things as they were.

That's why I know for sure that it was a crisp Christmas morning, the last spent in the flat, when Alexander ripped away impatiently at his largest present and let out a yell of delight on finding that it was his first, very own personal computer.

2

Moving to Independency

This time it was Natty who was afraid of the trees. After years of gazing at immobile patrician palaces with stony turrets, securely grounded in a bed of unyielding cobblestones, the sight of an overgrown hedge of conifers swaying and bending ferociously in a storm just outside her bedroom window was indeed a frightening experience.

A thin strip of virgin rainforest in the midst of suburbia, our garden with its impenetrable thicket and dense foliage could not be crossed without the aid of a compass and stout knife. The children adored it. They disappeared into the wilderness, made dens, hid in the trees and supplemented their picnics with fruit picked from the gnarled old apple trees. Meanwhile, Wolfgang and I spent the summer months knocking down walls, rebuilding them elsewhere and generally attempting to transform the shell of the house into a home, a challenge that we faced with lots of enthusiasm, less talent and little funding.

By the time we could turn our attention to the garden and realized that some of the wilderness would have to fall victim to the chainsaw, the children had become ardent nature lovers and formed a vociferous environmental pressure group. Alexander, Natty and Ben – each child sat defiantly on a branch in his or her favourite tree, chanting in unison: 'Save the trees! Save the trees!'

Tough negotiations followed. Tears were shed. But in the end we were allowed to clear the jungle in return for erecting a tree house at the end of the garden.

When the children weren't busy fighting for the rights of flora and fauna, they found plenty of other stimulating interests in our new surroundings. It was the small things about our house that we loved best; the letter box, for instance. After years of having to run down (and then back up) five flights of stairs to fetch the mail, it was nothing short of luxury to have our very own box sunk into the wall next to our front door. The postman opened a flap on the outside, dropped the delivery down a metal chute and we fished it out on the inside. Wolfgang made a little wooden door with a knob to cover the aperture, and the children sat on the stairs, waiting enchantedly for the morning post and the delight of tugging open the door and examining the incoming mail.

Doors, or rather hinges, fascinated Alexander. One day I walked into the kitchen and found him standing there, brow knotted with concentration, oblivious to everything around him except the new units. Slowly and deliberately he was opening the cupboard doors, observing intently the way the hinges moved to allow the door to be swung back 180 degrees. He repeated the action several times. Suddenly the pensive frown gave way to a look of deep satisfaction, a smile flickered over his face, he shut the door, straightened up and jumped with surprise at finding me in the room. 'Now I know how it works,' he volunteered contentedly and ran outside to play.

An eye for detail combined with great tenacity made Alexander a formidable opponent in games too. Strategy games were his favourites. He did not like losing. When, at the beginning, he was not the winner, he analysed the situation, studied the wheels, cards or bricks until he understood the mechanics of the game, and then, armed with this superior knowledge, beat us all mercilessly every time. He left nothing to chance.

These principles he applied with even more fervour to his latest obsession – the computer. It was one passion he shared with his dad. If Wolfgang hadn't decided to be a teacher, he would have been the born engineer. Machines of all shapes and sizes fascinate him, and he has a knack of being able to coax the most stubborn radio, photocopier or camera back to life. The pair of them would spend hours together poring over cables, deftly wielding screwdrivers, totally absorbed in earnest discussion of hardware and software details.

Already, with only a minimum of instruction from his father, he was a competent and creative programmer, able to identify the salient points quickly and turn theory into practice. Troubleshooting frustrated him, but once he had given vent to his anger, he was back at the keyboard, trying out new methods, searching for a solution to the problem and not giving up until he had resolved it, no matter how long it took.

Laudable though these character traits might be, they were also suffused with a certain arrogance and lack of altruism which sometimes clouded the family's relationship with Alexander, resulting in frequent verbal feuds and a sensitively huffy young boy.

Work on the house in that first summer occupied all our thoughts and time. Alexander had started grammar school, Ben primary that autumn and the year passed quickly with no family holiday. Once the worst of the back-breaking work was over, I decided to take 11-year-old Alexander on a two-week trip to Britain in an attempt to compensate him for parental neglect. Bursting with enthusiasm, he helped me plan a route, choose destination activities and count the days until we departed.

It was his first visit to London. Alexander stared at the crown jewels, navigated us out of the Hampton Court labyrinth, fed the pigeons and had several pertinent questions to ask about astrology after we had visited the Planetarium. We travelled north to Edinburgh. I showed him where he had listened to literature seminars at the university as an unborn babe, the turn-of-the-century tenement block where we used to live and imparted so many more half-shared embryonic memories that he fell asleep, exhausted, on a two-hour bus tour of the city.

On the flight home he fingered his food tray thoughtfully as I outlined plans for taking Natty and Ben on similar trips when they reached the same age. 'When I'm grown up,' he told me, 'I want to live in Britain. I want to be an Englishman in England.' He thought a bit more. 'This trip was great. When you've taken Natty and Ben, you could start with me again, you know. I'll be 16 then. I'd like that,' he added wistfully. 'I'd like that very much.'

As the children grew older, the annual family trips to Britain centred more around exploring cities. One year we discovered Lincoln.

Approaching it from the west, we could make out from afar its singular skyline of Minster, windmill and castle jutting out of an otherwise flat countryside like a shark's fin. We found a convenient parking place on the outskirts – our secret car park, we called it – only a short walk past the Toy Museum and the castle ramparts to the main square and narrow lanes with their quaint little shops.

After the initial visit, there was never any discussion about where we would go first. It was an unspoken rule that we would hurry over the cobbles, paying scant attention to the Minster gardens or castle forecourt (that would come later on the agenda) and that we wouldn't even stop to peek into the window of Brown's Pie Shop, because the children knew we would go there for lunch and treat ourselves to traditional home-made English pies. They ran excitedly down the narrow pavement of the aptly named 'Steep Hill' before vanishing abruptly through a shop door. By the time we parents had caught up, the three of them were comfortably ensconced – often sitting on the floor – in a musty-smelling, book-crammed, shelf-bursting maze of a bookshop that we knew and loved as 'The Reader's Rest'.

Alexander saved his pocket money for the better part of the year for these visits. Here were books, rows and rows of them, so many that you had to hold your breath in order to pass oncoming browsers, and, best of all, they fell within his purchasing power as they were nearly all second hand. Of course he could have bought them elsewhere too. But he loved the smell and intimate atmosphere of *this* bookstore.

Natty and Ben would make their selections in a reasonable time frame and itched to go for lunch. Alex we could never winkle out: his shopping list ran to several pages. From the age of 12, his myriad reading interests diversified further to include classic science fiction. Arthur C. Clarke was his favourite author and a missing title in his collection caused him agony, whilst tracking down a long sought after book afforded him immense pleasure. When, after repeated assurances of a return visit the following year, he finally left the premises with a deep sigh of regret, he stumbled up the hill clutching bags of reading material to add to his beloved and extensive personal library.

Alexander began collecting cities as enthusiastically as books. School trips widened his horizon and we filled in the odd geographical gap ourselves. Cambridge in England, but also Prague, Budapest, Paris and Rome, Alexander visited them all. As a young teenager in the company of his parents, he feigned indifference and dragged along behind us, pretending to have nothing to do with us, but when we discussed details of our guided tours afterwards, he couldn't help but enrich the conversation with such qualified remarks that we realized shamefacedly he had in fact paid more attention to the tour guide than anyone else.

We were relieved that he enjoyed travelling. Although we admired his computer talents – at 13 he had programmed a businessman's organizer, and by 15 he was selling his own computer games on a regular basis to a national magazine – we worried about our son being cooped up with his monitor for long periods in a room often ignorant of sunshine and birdsong and human laughter.

It was a bone of contention that we gnawed at incessantly. Sometimes we felt that Alexander was in danger of turning into a recluse. By nature not a gregarious type, he thrived on just a couple of close friends; parties and discos were not his scene. Physically, he was changing from a little boy to a young man with breathtaking speed.

Occasionally he complained about pains in his knees. Despite numerous examinations, no cause could ever be established. The doctors put it down vaguely to growing pains, and grow he certainly did. Soon he towered over me; a tall, slim boy with long legs that steadfastly refused to be contained within normal sized trousers.

Those were the awkward years. Give him a knotty problem on a topic he found interesting, and he would stay with it until he had solved it. Offer him a challenge in an area that he hated – Latin, for instance – and he would sink into stubborn inertia. There were ugly scenes in the mornings before school when I insisted on testing his Latin vocabulary, knowing full well that he had not learnt the day's quota. Alexander sat upright and defiantly on the chair opposite me, lips curled back in a sneer over his brace-imprisoned teeth, making no effort to cooperate. Twice he nearly failed the grade. Twice he scraped through.

So we were pleasantly surprised when he agreed to our suggestion that he should join the local rowing club and allot one afternoon a week to outdoor sport. Whilst the other members embarked on rigorous training sessions for regattas and contests, Alexander found genuine relaxation and enjoyment simply rowing along the quiet backwaters and tributaries of the Danube, sometimes alone, sometimes with a good friend, a development that struck us as more than positive. We worried less about him, but more about Natty.

She's such a *sensible* girl, people would say. Fun loving, empathetic, more outward going than her older brother, a trifle too conscientious about her schoolwork, she found harmony in music. When she was at home, the house hummed to the sound of *Summertime Blues* or *The Pink Panther* as she played the tunes deftly and passionately on the electric organ we had given her. But with the onset of puberty, the house frequently winced with disharmony.

These were difficulties we had not encountered with adolescent Alexander. Like many other girls of her age, Natty tested the limits to see how far she could go. Yet there was something not quite right, something we couldn't put our finger on.

The series of disturbing incidents grew in volume. Friends consoled us with hair-raising narratives of their teenage daughters' exploits and reassured us that Natty was certainly a little 'difficult', but nothing that could not be attributed to hormone changes. We allowed ourselves to be persuaded.

If she couldn't go out with friends in the evening, our intelligent, sensible and imaginative daughter would clock up long hours spent in front of the television, watching films that invariably seemed to deal with wayward daughters who got into bad company and came to sticky ends. She wanted to experiment. But instead of slowly drawing conclusions from her experiences and learning from her successes or failures, she vacillated more and more to excess behaviour. Even more worrying was her apparent inability to differentiate between reality and a fantasy world.

But for all the arguments and disagreements, the tears and, even worse, her bouts of total and crippling apathy, I never had the impression that the parent–child bond was severed. Beneath it all, I could still feel my child. Could, until one day when she was fifteen.

The phone call came late at night. We were asked to come to the hospital as soon as possible. Whilst away at a holiday camp, Natty had – for reasons not yet fully understood – swallowed a number of sleeping tablets and been admitted to hospital for treatment. Her condition was not serious, we were told, more of a cry for help (did we know if she had a boyfriend problem?), and the hospital envisaged a discharge in the morning.

Everything turned into a blur. Guilt at not having noticed her distress enveloped us. We were shocked at what had happened, relieved at the outcome and frightened and confused about what steps to take next.

When the hospital authorities suggested taking her to see a psychiatrist (just to be on the safe side, she's only a little mixed up), we agreed immediately.

For six months, the psychiatrist worked with Natty and us in his dim basement practice. Even in the first session we parents were astonished to find ourselves confronted with serious accusations, never ever formulated by Natty, ranging from alleged sexual abuse by her father to the revelation that Natty's induced birth suggested a neurotic tendency on my part to cling. My request that he might offer us his expert opinion on how to cope with our daughter today and tomorrow was however flatly refused.

Finally he made a devastating diagnosis. Our delightful, friendly and talented daughter was suffering from a severe personality disorder called Borderline Syndrome. She also showed signs of addictive behaviour. The cause of the illness remains controversial. Patients with this mental illness experience a wide range of symptoms of which the most tangible include self-mutilation, depression, substance abuse and suicidal tendencies. No cure exists, although the name suggests to the uninitiated that, with a modicum of determination and a heap of love, it should be possible to bring the sufferer back from the brink. As the years pass, the condition may improve – or may not.

In our helplessness, we agreed that Natty should continue to receive treatment. For another year she went to the psychiatrist twice a week, before terminating the sessions of her own accord.

We struggled. Struggled to comprehend that this was happening to our daughter and our family. Struggled to understand why. Struggled to map out a new code of co-existence that would accommodate Natty's illness and not cause her undue strain, as she reacted badly to stressful situations. And struggled most of all to rebuild our shattered self-confidence.

Hardly anyone outside the family had realized anything was amiss. Attempts to explain quickly revealed our own inadequacies and misguided conceptions of mental illness. Natty's neat physical appearance with no sign of a tendency to dribble, her intelligent conversation in grammatically correct sentences and unremarkable behaviour in the presence of guests seemingly belied the popular image of the mentally ill. When you cannot point at broken bones or specify pulled ligaments or clarify medical details with a quick visual doodle on a notepad, but must refer constantly to nebulous neural transactions, the result is rarely convincing.

In the meantime, Alexander was growing in leaps and bounds. In the course of a youth-hostelling trip in England with his schoolfriend Philipp, he had fallen head over heels in love. Excessive computer sessions gave way gracefully to walks in the park and back seats in the cinema. Tall, elegantly dressed and with an infectious laugh, he sauntered down the road hand in hand with his girlfriend, dreaming of the future they would share.

On completing school, his status as a German national required a year's military or civilian service. Alexander opted for the latter, informing us pointedly that he wished to gain independence by leaving home and carrying out his duty in Hamburg, a geographical half-way stop before then commencing studies – computer science – at Warwick University in England.

Now he was there, our 19-year-old son, on the threshold of his ambitions. An eloquent, independently minded young man, well versed in literature and philosophy, blessed with an incorrigible curiosity and dogged perseverance, a talent for witticisms, still shy in the company of strangers and not overly generous in his financial dealings with others, strictly opposed to drinking and smoking, with a proven track record in practicalities such as cooking lasagne, ironing, washing and driving a car.

So it was with great excitement that we helped our fledgling transport his books, computers and CDs to a room in a residential home for patients with multiple sclerosis, where Alexander would work as an assistant nurse along with regular staff and other lads of his age. Sitting on the edge of his bed in his new surroundings, legs swinging with pure delight, freed at last from the bondage, social and pecuniary, of family life and reunited with his girlfriend who had moved north with him, life seemed sweet indeed. 'Mum, don't forget to take your mug to the kitchen and wash it up,' came the poignant reminder of the role reversal now achieved.

When he came home for the occasional weekend visit, he bubbled over with vitality untainted by the harrowing plight of many of the patients, all severely handicapped, some totally paralysed, lying help-lessly in their beds until death should release them. Alexander was not impervious to their suffering, but his life pivoted around his girlfriend, new circle of friends and the delirious excitement of waking up in the morning as a citizen of a vibrant European city.

There were warning signs. After a few months, he seemed restless, snapped at us without provocation and displayed little appetite on home visits. But he would admit to no problems and he lived far removed from us. Coping with Natty's erratic behaviour had perhaps accustomed us to emotional upsets, so when the news broke that his girlfriend had sepa-rated from him, we empathized, but no doubt underestimated the impact this loss would have on him.

His boss sent him home on sick leave for ten days. Painfully thin, severely depressed and gripped with pain as only his intense personality could suffer, he allowed himself to be cared for and pampered by us all. He wept openly and shocked us by the depth of his emotions. No amount of discussion or listening or cuddling could relieve his distress.

'Something has snapped,' he repeated numbly. 'Something has just – snapped.'

Nevertheless, he elected to return to work as planned and, although his grief remained, we felt that he was making progress and beginning to explore new avenues. Yet seeing him for the first time after the break-up in his working environment in the home was a revelation. Alexander's relationship with the patients in his care had intensified. He identified with their fate to a degree that struck me as, well, unhealthy. Suddenly the thought shot through my mind – I hope *he* is not incubating some fatal disease. Please no. Not Alexander as well.

Four months later he had completed his service in the home. We knew he continued to pine for the estranged girlfriend, suspected that he was actively seeking a reconciliation, yet we also registered a rekindling of interest in the world about him and a sense of exhilarated anticipation concerning the imminent move to England.

We decided on one last family holiday together. Alexander agreed enthusiastically. By selecting a self-catering holiday cottage near the university, we intended to solve some of our son's logistic problems in transporting his now extensive household to his new abode, and at the same time explore the area where he would be living for the next three years.

To mark the occasion, I lashed out on a fourteenth century house with uninterrupted views over Kenilworth Castle and grounds. Cosy, if not spacious, the only drawback was the low doorframes. Wolfgang, Alexander and Ben suffered from repeated cranial collisions with the wooden beams so that we found ourselves investing less in ice creams and more in sticking plasters and cold compresses.

From the start, the campus university captivated Alexander. Surrounded by open countryside, the modern buildings and excellent facilities appealed to many a fresher. We admired his room in the halls of residence, located the computer science department, visited Coventry and found pub food that Alexander loved.

But in the holiday home, a dirty mug once again sparked off an emotional controversy about our respective roles. I felt aggrieved at being relegated to a domestic of the lowest orders, especially whilst on vacation, and insisted that the person – Alexander – who had simply abandoned the used cup in the living room should clean it. Alexander retorted that he was an adult and would do as he pleased. 'I am not a slave,' he said indolently. Neither was I. His imperiousness played on my nerves. It was time to let him go and live his own life.

We had come full circle. By settling in Coventry, not far from my home town of Cheltenham, Alexander provided a fresh link to our roots.

I think he was relieved too when we said goodbye at the end of the holiday. Polite as always, he kissed us, promised faithfully to write and phone and eat mountains of vegetables and change his socks and not overspend, waved cordially from the door, and disappeared inside before we had even turned the corner. So that was all right.

He settled down quickly. His letters, not infrequent, told of parties he attended, his delight at befriending fellow students from an eclectic mix of nationalities, the cultural activities and the feeling of being the right person in the right place at the right time. Gone were the depressions arising from jilted love, gone too, it would seem, his natural reservation in company. He blossomed and matured and embraced the future.

The e-mail arrived in November, two months into his first term at university. It was short and simple. 'Mum, Dad,' it began. 'I have to tell you. There is something wrong.'

3

Back to Square One

The annual ritual of preparing a traditional Christmas pudding in good time, and solemnly adding a silver coin to the dough whilst making secret and fervent wishes, had arisen more from necessity than inclination. Unable to purchase this icon of British food in Germany, I had no choice but to make it myself.

Loath to exclude Alexander from this early December tradition, we enrolled the aid of one of Ben's friends. Slightly bewildered by the whole procedure but keen to participate anyway, he screwed up his eyes, thought deeply for a moment and then with a dramatic sweep of his arm flung Alexander's coin into the mixing bowl.

'I wish Alexander a happy Christmas and hope he gets all the presents he wants,' he muttered, scrutinizing us anxiously afterwards to see if he had done right. Everyone laughed good-naturedly. That was just perfect, we reassured him. Now Alexander was certain to enjoy Christmas.

Or would he? After the initial fright of that e-mail, informing us that he had woken one morning in his bed and the next thing he knew he was lying on the floor near the washbasin with a bruised head and a searing pain in his knee with no recollection of what had happened, we had shrugged off the whole incident.

A check-up with the doctor had produced no results; Alexander's fear that he might have suffered an epileptic fit proved unfounded. The most likely explanation was that he had blacked out – tall, thin, young men such as Alexander must expect the odd circulation problem – and had cracked his head and knee while falling. Come back if it happens again, the doctor had said. But it didn't. Only the pain in his knee, just a throb really, nothing to fuss about, refused to go away. Alexander was receiving massage and surely that would do the trick.

What with all the usual seasonal round of cooking, baking, deciding on Christmas presents, writing cards and letters, inviting sceptical friends for mince pies on Advent Sunday afternoons, preparing festive events for my classes and redecorating Ben's old bedroom to serve as a guest room for Alexander's imminent flying visit, I was too preoccupied to give the matter further thought. When interrogated on the phone, Alexander would reply non-committally that his knee still hurt somewhat, that he was still receiving massage, and then abruptly changed the subject.

Not even the news that the doctor was at a loss to understand why the pain was not reacting to treatment and had referred Alexander to a specialist at a hospital in Birmingham perturbed me unduly. By the time a date had been set, shortly before the university Christmas holidays, Alexander was telling us that he didn't feel like going through with the appointment, as it all seemed so unnecessary.

When he arrived home on 15 December – via Hamburg – I hadn't finished writing all the Christmas cards or choosing all the little surprises for three stockings and still had two more days of teaching to get through.

He looked awful. Pale and emaciated. His left knee was grotesquely swollen, transfixing his leg permanently at an uncomfortable angle of 120 degrees. Lacklustre and apathetic, he withdrew to his bed in the freshly decorated 'little room' as we now called it, fed himself on the painkillers the doctor had given him and refused to move.

If we wanted to do something, we had to hurry. Over the Christmas period, surgeries and outpatient departments would be closed or running on a skeletal staff. I persuaded Alexander to stand up – he winced with pain – and allow me to drive him to our GP's surgery, if only to replenish the almost empty packet of painkillers.

The kindly old doctor, who had known the children all their lives, did not like what he saw. Need to have a closer look at this, young man, he told Alexander, swiftly plunging a needle into the angry, bulbous growth to take a probe, thereby unwittingly subjecting his patient to such intense pain that the latter screamed and nearly fainted. Clearly shocked, the doctor promised to get in touch as soon as the lab results came through.

Alexander went back to bed. Worry set in. I began to wonder whether this unidentified ailment would require surgery. Would there be time before Christmas?

After the last Christmas party with my students, I decided to take action. Natty had come to the same conclusion. Patiently, she sat on the edge of her brother's bed and told him – with considerable conviction – that something was clearly wrong and that he would be doing himself no favour by procrastinating. No doubt she had worn down his resistance, because when I walked into his room, summoning up all the residual maternal authority I possessed, and told him that I was taking him to hospital now whether he liked it or not, he did not object.

He dressed and limped downstairs. He sat on the chest of drawers where as a child he had stored mittens, scarves and woollen hats, wriggling his foot into his black leather shoe. He could not bend his leg far enough to reach the shoelace. I tied it up for him.

The doctor at the outpatient department said little. He wanted a CAT scan carried out immediately at a nearby centre and supplied Alexander with a pair of turquoise-coloured crutches sporting red reflectors on the handles. In our hypertension we thought that hysterically funny and roared with nervous laughter at the idea of Alexander hobbling around outside in the dark with flashing crutches.

By the time the scans were ready, consultation hours at the hospital had finished. We had to bide our time until the following morning. Alexander waited until I had bent down to tie up his shoelaces before blurting out: 'The doctor thinks I've got cancer.' He watched my face carefully for the reaction.

I was unprepared. On one level I still believed in a mechanical injury as a result of the fall. On another level of consciousness I sensed something much more sinister. Yet I rushed to deny his statement with exhortations not to jump to conclusions, wait for the results, tests are sometimes wrong and anyway it would all come out in the wash. Alexander said nothing.

I dropped him off at the entrance to the hospital, watched him limp painfully on his crutches through the revolving door and then drove off in search of a parking space. There were none. I cruised slowly around the square. But within minutes Alexander reappeared, a sheaf of papers wedged precariously under his arm. Drive to the next hospital, he told me expressionlessly. They are expecting me. There's an expert there who knows all about this.

This time we were in luck. I found a parking space immediately. Locating the surgical outpatient department in the hospital – a large and sprawling complex only a few hundred metres from our house, but on the other side of the motorway – proved equally straightforward. Clusters of bored people, some with limbs incarcerated in plaster casts, others in wheelchairs, many with walking aids, waited on stylish wooden benches, flicking restlessly through magazines and casting anxious glances at the door leading to the examination rooms. Alexander sat down while I announced his arrival at the desk. We expected a lengthy wait. We didn't talk.

Once again, I was unprepared. Almost immediately, a voice on the loudspeaker called Alexander's name. Everything went so quickly that it didn't even occur to me to ask if he wanted me to accompany him. A few people watched with mild curiosity as he picked his way alone over to the door.

I tried to read an article in one of the magazines, but found I couldn't concentrate. Facing me on the wall was a series of posters showing in graphic detail how surgical know-how and a copious amount of titanium can often replace bones ravaged by cancer, thus avoiding amputation in many cases. I looked the other way.

To my intense relief, Alexander came back out after a short while. This seemed to me a good omen. If something was really wrong, he would surely have been in there for hours. His facial expression revealed nothing. 'We can go home,' he told me in a matter-of-fact tone. But of course. I'd known all along that this knee business was a nuisance and nothing more. Back to the GP, I thought, remembering that we had not yet received the lab results.

Alexander looked straight into my eyes.

'We're going home. It's cancer. Bone cancer. We have to go home, pick up my things and come straight back. They want to do an exploratory operation – a biopsy – tomorrow, but the consultant has already told me that there is not a shade of doubt in his mind that I have an osteosarcoma.' He appeared calm and unconcerned, relieved even.

Osteosarcoma. I rolled the word around in my head. It presented itself to me in three distinct parts. 'Osteo', I remembered from school Latin, meant something to do with bones. Visions of the rugged, solitary isle of Sark came to mind when I thought of the next segment 'sarc'. That left 'oma', the German vernacular word for 'granny'. Yes, that's how you had to imagine it: a colony of senior citizens curing their rickety bones on a peaceful island. This osteosarcoma didn't sound threatening at all. A puffed-up knee? Nobody dies – dies? – of a swollen knee. That's the kind of affliction that calls for cold packs and deep-healing creams, cuddles and perhaps – but only perhaps – a story from Volume Four.

Little did I know that while sarcomas account for only 2 per cent of all cancers they are dreaded for their aggressiveness and poor prognosis. Of the various and rare bone cancers, osteosarcoma is the most common, befalling annually three victims in a million inhabitants, predominantly young people between the ages of 10 and 25, slightly more males than females. Typically, the primary tumour occurs in the bone above the knee or arm joint. It spreads quickly and eagerly. Even at an early stage, secondary tumours or metastases are common in the lungs and brain.

I looked at Alexander. A denial process set in. I needed time to think. Let's not jump to conclusions, I warned. They haven't even taken a tissue sample yet. Modern medicine is wonderful, but they don't always get everything right. Even if it is a tumour, it is much more likely to be benign. But my voice trailed away unconvincingly.

Outside the hospital, the world looked much the same as it had just half an hour previously. Only for us nothing would ever be the same again.

Stunned and shaken, I drove us home. On reflection, we decided that an hour or two would make no difference and we might as well cook ourselves some lunch before returning to the hospital. I helped Alexander with his shoes and tripped over his crutches, these unfamiliar accessories and constant reminder of his unfolding fate.

I went to considerable trouble preparing that lunch. Partly out of a desire to please him, cheer him up, fortify him, partly because I laboured under the illusion that he had been neglecting his diet, which had somehow contributed to his cancer, and that all I had to do now was offer him nutritious fare for the situation to be reversed.

The others came home after school for lunch. With carefully chosen wording designed to be honest but not overly dramatic, we explained that the consultant suspected cancer and wanted Alexander in hospital. There was silence at the table. Apart from Alexander himself, whose appetite had returned, everybody else played with their knives and forks and healthy food.

We packed a small bag with essentials – reading material mostly, and then as an afterthought, pyjamas and toothbrushes – and drove back to the hospital. We couldn't find a parking space so had to leave the van further down the road and then hobble all the way back. Already Alexander's hands showed red weals from gripping the crutches.

Back in the surgical department, we were asked to wait in a corridor. Alexander's leg stuck out in front of the chair. He was preoccupied trying to prevent passers-by tripping over it. Every now and then someone arrived to interview him and jot down his answers. To save him the trouble of walking over to the administration and standing in a lengthy queue, I volunteered to do it for him.

The health service in Germany works differently from that in Britain. Residents are obliged to take out a health insurance policy with either a state registered company, or opt for private insurance. Because teachers have civil service status, part of their health costs is borne by the State; the remainder must be covered by private insurance. Just like at Alexander's birth, I found myself floundering with unfamiliar phrases and expressions that I had not yet encountered and most certainly did not endear myself in my confusion and distress to the staff member dealing with our forms.

On my return, I found Alexander repeating, with growing exasperation, the information he had already given to the last three interviewers. The staff behaved neutrally, occasionally over-cheerfully. From a safe distance they watched us silently, commiseration and sadness in their eyes.

A doctor from the ward waiting to admit Alexander introduced himself. He was kind, sat down with us and chatted easily. On discovering that Alexander was half British, he confessed to being a passionate admirer of British films and actors. He wanted to know who our favourites were. We stared at him blankly. Try as I might, I could not think of the name of one single film or actor. Neither could Alexander. The word 'Oscar' kept turning into 'osteosarcoma'.

Finally a bed was ready on the ward and Alexander invited to occupy it. Two other older men shared the room. They nodded politely in greeting and, seeing the crutches, asked whether Alexander had broken his leg, perhaps while playing football? When he told them quite openly, no, he had cancer, the conversation came to a halt. They looked away in embarrassment.

Once the steady stream of nurses wanting blood samples had dried up, Alexander dismissed me, making a point of telling me that he could manage quite well on his own, thank you, and really did not need or want me fussing around. I drove home obediently.

An emergency case brought to the operating theatre the following morning delayed all the following operations. By lunchtime, Alexander was still on the ward, peevish and extremely thirsty, as he was not allowed to drink. Not until late in the evening did his turn come. I promised to be there when he returned to the ward, a gesture that he rejected as being completely unnecessary.

As we had understood it, the surgeon wanted to extract a sample of the tumour. This would then be sent to the laboratory where it could be identified within a week. We had gained the impression that the biopsy itself entailed only minor surgery. Thinking that it would all be over in an hour or so, I returned to the ward only to be told that the operation was taking longer than expected. It was late by now. The hospital was deserted. I walked past the closed doors of the patients' rooms to the entrance hall and sat down on a bench next to a magnificent Christmas tree, elegantly decorated with baubles and lights. I waited a long time.

The nurse suggested I go home, promising to ring as soon as she had any news. I was too tired to argue, and as it was nearly midnight I took her advice.

At home, Wolfgang and I waited some more. Eventually the phone call came, informing us that Alexander was out of theatre, but had lost a lot of blood and as a result was feeling poorly.

We hardly recognized our son when we visited first thing the next day. He was white. The bed was white. He was wearing a white operating gown. His leg was wrapped in generous layers of white bandages. It was propped up in a white cradle to prevent it from slipping. An infusion stand stood next to his bed. A drip drained into his arm. A urine bottle hung at the side of the bed. And he groaned with pain whenever we accidentally brushed against the bed.

In the course of the next five days we discovered that Alexander had a long wound which ran over the knee joint and was held together with ten stitches. For his part, the surgeon had made the discovery that the tumour, which was growing from the inside of the bone out, had hollowed out the femur – the thighbone – to the extent that it could fracture. Alexander was warned not to put any weight on that leg. Weak as he was, he could not walk anyway.

Only one thing was certain: Alexander would need to undergo a further test called 'staging'. A magnetic resonance image – MRI – would reveal any other secondary growths in the body.

Relief. The pictures showed no trace of any metastases. We knew that his chances of survival would have dropped dramatically with the detection of more cancer cells.

Information was not readily forthcoming. Several times we were consoled with the promise of round-table talks with representatives from both the surgical and oncological departments. But nothing happened. Despite our repeated requests for details, we received only vague hints of an impending amputation and chemotherapy. When and whether Alexander could be discharged remained a mystery.

So it came as a total surprise to hear at lunchtime on Christmas Eve that Alexander was being sent home there and then by ambulance. After Christmas he would be readmitted, we were told. They would phone us with the dates.

Once again, we were unprepared. My GP had shut his surgery for a fortnight's Christmas break, nobody had explained how or where we might find a home care nurse, and the hospital simply supplied us with a prescription for painkillers that we had to take to a chemist's on emergency call on the other side of town because the shops had all closed at lunchtime for the three-day Christmas break.

Without Alexander's knowledge gleaned from his work in the residential home, we would not even have realized that we needed other aids for home care as well. A bed pan for instance, urine bottles, a raised toilet seat and, oh yes, a hospital bed. Miraculously, Wolfgang succeeded in tracking down these artefacts and arranging for them to be delivered before the day was out.

Christmas we spent hunched up in Alexander's tiny room. Syringes, bandages and bottles of medicine outnumbered presents and stocking fillers by a ratio of three to one. We took it in turns to sit with Alexander and keep him company. I learned how to dress the wound without making him scream too much with pain.

Silence reigned. We waited for the phone call from the hospital. There had been no further contact or information.

Everything was confusing and strange. We were frightened and had any number of questions. So when we were finally given an appointment with one of the senior doctors in oncology and told that she would put us in the picture, our expectations for this first meeting ran high.

Wolfgang and I drove without Alexander but with his consent to discuss his case to the hospital. The conversation was disappointing. The doctor made her displeasure clear at having been obliged to interrupt her short holiday because of us, teachers to boot, who were always on holiday. My request for information such as patient's leaflets, contact addresses and self-help organizations took her by surprise. She pointed out curtly that that was not her responsibility and added haughtily that there was nothing to stop me consulting a psychiatrist if I thought I couldn't cope.

What a shame that exactly at that moment when patients and their relatives are struggling with overwhelming feelings of stress, shock and fear, they have to expend even more energy in order to find help.

Like others before us, we agonized over the vexed question of whether another hospital would offer superior treatment and, therefore, a higher survival rate. By checking out internet sites on the subject we discovered that each country follows a standard course of treatment, called a protocol, overseen by a central co-ordinator (in this case, the University of Hamburg) accessing a comprehensive database of cases and carefully adjusted in line with new research. Every hospital follows the central plan. That was a considerable relief, because we felt that living so near to the clinic offered us a considerable advantage.

By the time friends and family had become aware of our changed circumstances (we saw no point in disrupting their seasonal cheer and many were away on holiday), we had mutated into a different group of people. Once the initial numbing shock had subsided, we set about solving the many practical considerations. It helped keep our minds off the real issue.

Endless discussions ensued. How could we best reorganize our daily life? My first thoughts centred round my teaching commitments and the already booked study trip I was planning alone. Stop everything. Cancel the trip. At that stage, the financial loss would still be bearable.

But on reflection I came to the conclusion that this would hardly be advisable. Sitting next to Alexander 24 hours a day would only irk him and exhaust me. Quality rather than quantity seemed to be the motto. 'I want everything to stay as normal as possible,' Alexander intoned.

Yet more time had to be unlocked. I listed my usual occupations according to whether they seemed necessary or unnecessary. From that it soon became apparent that growing all my own flowers and vegetables from seed could be best dispensed with!

Family friends in Britain – Chris and Irene – kindly volunteered to collect Alexander's belongings from his halls of residence and store them in their house until further notice. The university quickly re-let his room, keeping overheads at a minimum. Alexander's Director of Studies suggested he might try to keep abreast of his work by submitting assignments by post. The first 'get well' cards arrived in the letter-box. I threaded them on a blue ribbon and hung them up from the ceiling in his room.

Alexander never threatened to refuse treatment, but he fought bitterly to retain the last vestiges of his independence, insisting petulantly that he had no need of our help and would in fact be better off in England with his friends caring for him. That rankled.

On 30 December the oncological department of the hospital rang us. The results were not yet back but they did not want to waste more time. It was imperative that treatment start within two weeks of the first – unfortunate – lancing of the tumour, as this might have encouraged cancer cells to spread through the bloodstream.

We called an ambulance. On New Year's Eve, Alexander had the dubious honour of being the first patient to be treated with the very latest protocol.

At midnight, Wolfgang and I walked out into the freezing, starry-skied night. A protracted cold spell had transformed the Danube into layers of ice, piled up like a deep-frozen potato gratin. Standing on the bridge with friends, we toasted in the New Year to the sound of the cathedral bells ringing and watched as the sky turned red with the light of millions of fireworks.

No, he hadn't seen them, Alexander confessed later. His bed had been facing the wrong way.

4

Life in Hospital

The corridor was dark and endlessly long. On the left and the right numerous grey doors. A solitary window provided, with more than a touch of architectural symbolism, a wan light at the end of the tunnel.

After the first night, Alexander was transferred to one of the two single rooms, a privilege that he had the nursing staff to thank for. They knew what we still had to discover: that the chemotherapy procedure would overtax any room-mate.

Next to the bed was the ubiquitous hospital trolley table with pull-out tray, drawer, locker and a parking space for the pre-installed telephone. In the corner of the room a wardrobe, and, suspended on a wall bracket on the opposite wall, a television. Once they had signed on the dotted line, patients could watch programmes of their choice by headphones only and at a small hourly charge. A calendar featuring Bavarian beer tankards, a small table, two chairs, a washbasin and a wall cabinet with a mirror behind a curtain completed the inventory.

The view through the window encompassed blocks of flats, the red brick chimney of a disused factory and, in the background, a snow-covered ridge of hills. With its north-facing position, the room attracted little sun. On the upside, it was quiet; patients in the south-facing rooms had to endure the ear-splitting noise of the motorway day and night.

The nursing staff consisted of a professor, who reigned as head of department, and under him two senior doctors, supported in turn by juniors who spent all of their working hours on the ward. Bringing up the vanguard was a team of nurses, trainee nurses, a couple of young men doing their civilian service and a cheery set of cleaners.

We soon learnt to appreciate and respect the people working on the ward. The nurses, some of them barely older than Alexander, tried hard to create a cosy atmosphere and took or made time for the youngest patient on the ward.

At last we knew where to turn with our questions – to the ward doctors. With her honest replies and calm manner, Dr P quickly won our trust and Dr S understood how to joke with Alexander despite the seriousness of the situation.

And he had news for us. The bad one first. The biopsy results had arrived and confirmed that not only was the tumour malignant, but that it belonged to the most aggressive subgroup called a telangiectatic osteosarcoma. The very last loophole had gone. Now all we could do was hope that the treatment would be successful.

Because the staging had not revealed any secondary growths, Alexander was not classified as a high-risk patient. According to the protocol, he was placed in the group receiving the standard treatment plan, which would kick-start with a blast of highly dosed and extremely toxic chemotherapy lasting about 48 hours, Dr S explained.

'In other words,' he added with a worried look, 'if we don't poison you, you might survive.' Alexander grinned.

Somewhat reluctantly Alexander signed the consent sheet, so agreeing that he had been informed about possible risks and side effects. The list was frighteningly long. The treatment could lead to sterility, kidney failure, irreversible long-term damage to the heart and impede his hearing. Up to as many as 10 per cent of cases contracted leukaemia at a later stage. During the therapy, most patients experienced violent sickness and nausea, mouth sores and severe constipation alternating with diarrhoea. Because the chemotherapy works by eradicating all new and fast-growing cells, benign or malignant, it also decimates the patient's white blood cells. As these are responsible for keeping up the body's immune system, there is a constant risk of a fatal infection. We would all have to take great care not to import germs, coughs or colds. Oh yes, and within two weeks, Alexander's hair would fall out.

Due to the sheer potency of the chemicals involved and the high risk of complications as a result, osteosarcoma patients are required to stay in hospital for the duration of the treatment, unlike many other cancer patients on less toxic protocols who can often opt for outpatient services.

Dr S also explained that Alexander would be exposed to ten weeks of pro-operative chemotherapy before the operation on his leg. The idea was to try and shrink the tumour first in the hope that, if the damage to the bone was not too extensive, the limb could be saved. To amputate or not to amputate? Nobody would be able to decide until shortly before-hand. If, and the doctor emphasized the word *if,* things went well, then the surgeon would remove the section of diseased bone and replace it with an endoprothesis – a metal rod connected to an artificial knee joint.

The doctor glanced at Alexander's swollen knee. He should be prepared for an amputation, he ventured, and talked quickly and rather vaguely about a 'little more' post-operative chemotherapy – just to be on the safe side.

Alexander looked small. Lying prostrate in bed disguised his height of 1.86 m. Dr S considered him thoughtfully.

'Look, Alexander. Your leg is not the problem. Better to lose a leg than die.' Alexander said nothing. We would hear that remark over and over again. Yet something was wrong with this seemingly logical argument. But what? Not until much later did I realize where the problem lay: Alexander needed time; lots of time to grieve and take leave of his leg. Being able to express his fears freely, and not having to listen to us brushing them aside like crumbs off a table but taking them seriously, was of paramount importance to him.

So now we knew. Dr S said goodbye and left. Alexander had two wishes. He asked me to buy him a large, bound notebook which he intended to use as a journal. And he wanted me to compile a photo-graphic documentary of the coming events so that afterwards he would be able to show his friends what he had been through.

I found that surprising. Previously this sensitive lad had been loath to appear on pictures. Did he have a foreboding that they could be the last pictures of him?

It started. The first bottle of chemotherapy had the same effect on me as cars: they come in different colours, have names I can never remember and either work or don't work. Over the next few months, whole rivers of chemicals in fetching hues of red, orange and yellow would surge into Alexander's body. He could always identify each and every one of them with its correct chemical name – tongue-twisters such as adriamycine, methotrexate, cisplatin or ifosfamid – and understood perfectly that it was the cunning mixture of different poisons ('Medicine, Alex, medicine, not poison, please,' the doctor corrected him) which would, it was hoped kill off the cancer cells.

From the drip in Alexander's arm, now bruised and angry-looking from all the needle pricking required for the endless blood tests, and up to the infusion bottle, the chemotherapy was monitored by an infusion machine. This livid green box clamped onto the drip stand checked automatically that no air bubbles had entered the system and regulated the speed with which the chemotherapy was dispensed. Too fast, and Alexander's life would be endangered.

Unfortunately, this concentrated piece of technology was prone to frequent breakdowns, accompanied by a piercing warning bleep. Every time it happened, Alexander rang for a nurse who appeared sooner or later to inspect the damage, sort out the problem, reset the machine and start it again. These interruptions lasted anything from five to thirty minutes. At the beginning it didn't seem so onerous. But over the week, it all added up.

What goes in, must come out. Theoretically, Alexander could have grabbed the infusion stand and pulled it along behind him whenever he wanted the toilet, but as he needed both arms for the crutches, he could only get up with outside help. He had to pee very often. As both the quantity and quality had to be checked carefully, he opted for the urine bottle solution. They hung chained to the side of the bed, just like its hapless occupant.

The initial round of chemotherapy produced some nausea, but nothing as bad as we had feared. Alexander was perky with a streak of arrogance. He arranged himself in his bed, faking the terminal patient, and ordered a photo session. Afterwards he sat as upright as possible and provocatively busied himself with reading *Nausea* by Jean-Paul Sartre.

He talked openly about losing his hair and suggested I bring him a headscarf and an eye patch.

'Whatever for?' I asked.

Alexander pulled back the blanket. 'Well, once they have my leg off, I'll make a pretty good pirate.'

On other occasions he insisted we went home and stopped fussing. (Were we fussing?) We were driving him mad and he didn't need us anyway, he could manage quite well on his own. Please try to remember that he was no longer a baby, but a young man of twenty.

At other times the conversation took a more constructive turn. A friend had given us a book called *The Healing Family* by Stephanie Simonton and the suggestions and techniques described there for the patients and their relatives struck me as interesting. Most intriguing seemed to be the visualization method, which encouraged the cancer patient to create an image of his or her tumour and then imagine the effect the chemotherapy is having on it.

Alexander sat up.

'That's easy. My tumour looks like a wild mushroom with a face and arms and legs. It's smiling at me and leaning on a spade. The chemotherapy is not bothering him at all. But I want to have a chat with this mushroom and see if we can't sort out the whole matter amicably. I think I'll suggest to him that I really quite like him, but tell him that he's standing on a rather inconvenient spot. Actually, it's damned painful. So maybe he wouldn't mind moving over a little.'

'Do you think that's, well, aggressive enough? I mean, I thought the idea was to zap the wretched thing, like in those computer games, not be nice to it.'

'I don't want to be horrible to it. I think it will work out better this way. And anyway, it's my tumour and my mushroom.' His voice suddenly grew louder.

'Okay. What's the spade for?'

Alexander did not hesitate for a moment.

'The mushroom is doing some gardening and he needs it for digging. He wants to plant some carrots.'

An expert would no doubt have found this story revealing. But for the whole hospital with its 750 beds, there was only one psychologist and he was on leave for the next six months. I could think of only one interpretation. Alexander was imagining his own grave.

Yet we did not talk openly about death. That possibility seemed so remote, so unreal. Our discussions revolved much more around the 'why' question.

Could there be a connection between my mother's cancer and Alexander's? We wondered whether Alexander's long-standing dislike of vegetables (apart from peas and carrots) could have had a detrimental effect. Finally we turned to the psychological aspects. No disagreement here. Without any shade of doubt, the trauma of separation from his girlfriend had left him severely depressed, attacking his immune system and leaving him susceptible to illness.

As the day wore on, Alexander began to feel distinctly poorly. No longer bristling with self-assurance, he lay pinned to the bed and looked the picture of misery. He had started to feel sick and be sick. His back hurt and he couldn't eat. Wolfgang and I sat with him in shifts, trying to distract our fractious son from the infusion.

We compiled a list of '101 things to do with your gallows', as the triangle hanging over the bed was fondly known as in German, and congratulated ourselves at coming up with 16 non-fatal ideas. Alexander liked the black humour.

When Dr S popped in to see how things were going, Alexander mentioned how glad he would be when it was finished and he could go home again. The doctor shifted uncomfortably from one foot to the other. He explained apologetically that even when the chemotherapy had run through as planned, it would still not be the end of the affair. He reminded us of the toxicity of the chemicals that would erode the kidneys unless flushed out with litres of saline infusions. Another 48 hours on the drip would be necessary.

This latest information rocked us. Had we not listened properly when the procedure was being explained to us? But there was no way out now. Alexander would have to endure another two days.

The pretty, orange-coloured fluid in the bottles gave way to a boring, translucent one. At regular intervals the infusion machine overheated and broke down. With the help of ice packs, the nurses coaxed it to continue for another couple of hours.

But eventually it was over. The doctor rang for an ambulance to take Alexander home and informed us that he would need a blood test every third day to check his white blood cell count. If it fell below 1000, the risk of an infection would increase dramatically; Alexander should come back to hospital at the first sign of a temperature or if he cut himself. Otherwise, he now had a week at home to recuperate.

Back within our own four walls, the family was on the brink of collapse from the strain of the last four days. Alexander was washed-out and desperately tired from lack of sleep and the constant need to pass water. He also complained of still feeling sick and of a strange taste in his mouth. But he was home, even if he didn't much appreciate the fact, and knowing that all my children were under one roof again gave me a strange sense of security.

School started again after the Christmas holidays. Standing in front of a class of strapping young men, with healthy legs and bursting with energy, was painful for me. All the groups chatted gaily about their holidays. The harmless banter added to my sense of isolation. I made the decision there and then not to announce Alexander's illness, not because I was afraid of breaking any taboos but rather because I needed a space to work in where life could still continue normally.

With the return to school, friends discovered gradually what had happened and the phone rang incessantly. Some could not conceal their shock. Some told me, no, if it happened to them, they wouldn't be able to cope. Others begged us to reconsider the choice of hospital and recommended clinics in every conceivable part of the country. Whenever a television programme featured new cancer cures, people phoned to tell us. Almost everybody knew of a relative, friend or colleague who – they claimed – had had osteosarcoma and survived. Others again asked if there was anything they could do to help.

To that I replied, yes, please just be normal to me. Please ring me, rather than waiting for me to ring you – I don't have the stamina to reach for the phone, and anyway the many calls, national and international, were slowly crippling us financially. Please don't be offended if you invite us to the cinema and we accept, only to find we have to cancel at the last moment. Please be patient with us. Please don't leave us alone with this.

Towards the end of the week, the hospital rang Alexander to inform him that they would need him back for further tests and to fit him out with a central catheter, called a Hickmann, which would mean a small operation to implant the tube in his chest. This step was necessary for two reasons: first, because without it his veins would be literally eaten away by the acidity of the chemotherapy and, second, it would save him the torture, mental and physical, of constant needle pricks.

Alexander was hostile to the idea. He felt hemmed in. He had lost the control over his body and now for the first time sensed a chance to demonstrate his independence. For two days he kept up a stubborn resistance. Then it crumbled away.

So the second round of hospital commenced with another session in the operating theatre and ended with an ugly, painful gash over his right collar bone and, protruding from a hole in his chest, a tube which could be used to hook him up directly to the drip.

This time the bottles gleamed yellow. The chemo dripped placidly down and disappeared into Alexander's chest, accompanied by the rhythmic whine and hum of the pump. Sometimes the effect was soporific.

We settled down to family shifts for visiting Alexander. In the morning I looked in for two hours. Natty and Ben shared another two hours in the afternoon and Wolfgang kept his son company in the evening. We wanted to support Alexander but not smother him.

Sitting with him in the little room was unbelievably strenuous. It made our bones ache. Every 20 minutes or so, he reached for the urine bottle and sent us out to wait in the corridor until he had finished. Despite antidotes, he was violently and repeatedly sick. His food lay untouched on the bedside table, the curtains remained drawn and this proud son, who had never liked hugging and cuddling, held my hand under the bedclothes and whispered words of thanks.

When he felt slightly better, we talked. We pictured all the pleasant things he would treat himself to once this chemotherapy was over. Alexander wished for a huge plate of English breakfast, followed by 24 hours of sleep, then a video session ('How about watching *Dead Man Walking*, Mum?'), then have a couple of friends round, and oh yes, it would be really neat if I could cook him kedgeree for lunch and then – he was sick again. So horribly sick that he forbade us to say the word F-O-O-D.

Two bleeping drips, one on the stand, the other fixed to the head of the bed, contributed to an acute lack of sleep and persistent exhaustion. Four weeks of inactivity gnawed away at the muscles in his legs. In contrast, the tumour-swollen knee appeared grotesquely large. At least the pain had all but disappeared.

One of the doctors tried to convince Alexander that cortisone would relieve the vomiting. Once again, Alexander railed and refused. As yet his need for self-determination outweighed his physical suffering. We started counting the days, the hours and the minutes. Anything to get out of here and go home.

But it turned out differently. No sooner had the chemotherapy and flushing stopped than the doctors decided Alexander had lost too much weight and hooked him up to a high-calorie infusion. Then a second one. And a third. Finally, they admitted that this would just merge with the next chemotherapy. After 170 hours non-stop on the drip, pale, gaunt Alexander was granted, as a token of goodwill, one hour of freedom in which to change his shirt, be helped out of bed into a wheelchair and go to the bathroom. Ten minutes of privacy.

The nightmare continued unabated. His hair started to fall out. Individual hairs at the beginning. Then whole tufts. They covered the sheet, itched and tickled. Alexander seemed unruffled by his imminent baldness. He asked the nurse to shave his head completely. That was the part I was dreading. Nothing symbolized cancer more realistically to me than the sight of hairless children. Now mine was about to join their ranks.

I had to agree with the nurse, nevertheless. My son was indeed blessed with a beautifully shaped head. No unsightly bumps or elongated curves. Altogether well proportioned. This head even sounded like my son, made noises like my son and claimed to be my son. But it took one lot of getting used to.

Alexander had learned that he could save valuable time and hasten the moment of discharge by mending the infusion machine himself whenever it broke down. More and more often though, the nausea prevented him from reacting. He lay there, immobile, huddled up in the corner of the bed in the dark room, wracked with violent spasms of pain in his leg that jerked the screams out of his lungs. Even a higher dose of painkillers did not seem to bring these attacks under control.

We were worried and distressed. What was going on? If the disappearance of pain just two weeks previously had brought hope and comfort, now we staggered from one crisis to the next, convinced that the tumour was growing and not shrinking. It seemed the only possible explanation for the fresh waves of pain.

The vomiting left him shivering and exhausted. Our conversations were short, often non-existent. For hours I would sit next to his bed, holding his hand under the bedclothes.

It required a superhuman effort on everybody's part to get through those harrowing weeks. Our nerves were stretched to the limit. We tried to keep up Alexander's flagging spirit by painting word pictures of how we would spoil him silly when he came home and we calculated just how much longer that would be. To be on the safe side, we added a margin of 24 hours. The medical staff agreed that a discharge on Thursday was realistic.

So Alexander's excited phone call home on Sunday came as a total surprise. Apparently the doctors had said things were going so well that he could come home on Tuesday. Could that be true? But the good news received a second medical blessing in my presence. Nothing could hold us back now. We floated on cloud seven, dreamt about all the wonderful things we would do, all the meals we would have, the peace and sleep.

Wolfgang joined in the general spirit of happiness and started packing together Alexander's accumulated belongings and carrying them out piecemeal, to the cheers of the staff who watched benignly. Alexander was transformed. On a piece of paper he crossed out every hour that passed, monitored the progress of the last bottle impatiently and fretted about ordering an ambulance 45 minutes ahead of time.

The door opened. In came the ward doctor. He looked earnest. He sat down next to Alexander and fiddled with the files he had brought with him.

'I'm so sorry, Alexander, but I cannot discharge you yet. This stuff is lethal. We must watch your kidneys. You need at least another six litres of the saline infusion. That means it will take a bit longer. 24 hours. But you can go home tomorrow. It's only one more day,' he added reasonably.

We stared at him in disbelief. Alex came to his senses first.

'But you promised! We asked you and you said yourself I could go earlier. Do you mean to say you have been leading me up the garden path?'

The doctor admitted this was so, but defended the deed by saying it had all been in Alexander's best interests – everybody could see that he could not take any more. He honestly believed that a little white lie would do more good than harm.

For a moment Alexander was silent. Then all the pent-up pain, fear, distress and misery erupted.

'I don't care what you think! These are my kidneys, and I couldn't care less if they are damaged or not. All I want to do is get out of here and go home. You all lied to me. I think that's the most rotten, backhanded trick I've ever come across. Why are you doing this to me?' He burst into hot, broken-hearted sobs. It was the first time he had cried.

The doctor looked wretched. Everyone had only meant well and now… He tried to put things right by promising to get hold of the most reliable infusion machine in the hospital and apologizing profusely. Too late. Our trust had been betrayed; the feeling of security had gone. We had nothing to hold on to any more. Just a vacuum of uncertainty and deep mistrust.

If the staff had deceived us on this relatively harmless account, well, they would surely have no qualms in hoodwinking us on the serious matters.

The rest of the day passed in shell-shocked stupor. Nurses came and went on routine errands, but avoided our looks and scuttled away guiltily. True to his promise, the doctor produced a new, much quieter machine. But the atmosphere in the room was as poisoned as the chemotherapy. Alexander punished them all with silence.

On the following day, when the nurse announced the 'last' bottle, he showed no reaction. The doctor confirmed that he had already called for an ambulance. Alexander didn't so much as look at him. Dr S handed him a written timetable for the rest of the treatment up to the operation. A peace offering, a reconciliatory gesture. From now on, the truth, the whole truth and nothing but the truth.

The pump bleeped. We had waited so long for this moment. But again, Alexander showed no reaction.

The doctor freed Alexander from the drip, sealed the Hickmann line with a cap, handed me his letter of discharge, signed the therapy passbook, reminded us to have our GP carry out blood tests every three days and to bring Alexander back in two weeks. He shook our hands and said goodbye.

The ambulance men lifted Alexander carefully onto the stretcher and pushed him out into the corridor. Mechanically, I collected the last remaining bags and books and wandered out, still suspecting strongly that the men had sneaked Alexander back in through another door for another two weeks of chemotherapy. But they hadn't. I cycled home and arrived in time to watch the paramedics carry Alexander upstairs and deposit him in his hospital bed at home.

Suddenly it was all over. The nightmare of the last three weeks was actually over. But we were unable to enjoy it.

5

Life at Home

For the last one-and-a-half years Alexander had not lived under the same roof as us. I had become accustomed to spending the mornings when I wasn't teaching alone in the house. Now this luxury belonged to the past. Alexander lay upstairs in bed, day in, day out. Generally he slept, he caused me no trouble; but he was there.

Then all the unfamiliar smells and noises. Alexander was forced to go to the toilet several times a night. Where before silence had reigned, doors now banged shut and his crutches tapped on the wooden floor. Every so often in the middle of the night they would fall over, making a terrible din, and I would run downstairs in a fright to see if he had hurt himself.

The bookcase and cupboard in his room now accommodated nothing but medical supplies. Crammed full of bandages, disinfectants and pills, they lent the little room a tell-tale scent. Strategically spread around the house lay piles of mouth masks. All the familiar objects of our everyday life had been moved, muddled up or simply disappeared. It was very strange.

To start with, Alexander could not sleep; he missed the constant whine of the infusion pump in hospital. Food was the next challenge. The chemotherapy had played havoc with his taste buds, making sweet things appear abominably sweet and salty things abominably salty. Just to add to the misery, he complained of a sore mouth, chronic constipation and a lingering feeling of nausea.

Apart from the isolated eating binge in hospital, Alexander had barely touched any food and his weight had plummeted – despite the high calorie infusions – from his already insubstantial 65 kg to a worrying 56 kg. Before the doctors can give the go-ahead for the next round of chemotherapy, the patient has to fulfil several conditions: blood and urine samples must be on target, no sign of an infection, no raised temperature over the last 48 hours and no less than a 25 per cent weight loss. There was little time to catch up. Alexander was under considerable pressure – mentally and physically.

He worked out his own dietary scheme, adapting it as necessary and willingly keeping in mind the doctor's advice not to worry about healthy foodstuffs, but simply to stuff in as much food as possible. Dr P had assured him that the body takes what it needs, so he should eat whatever he fancied. He fancied banana milkshakes. They formed the transition from chemotherapy to solid foods. When they began to stay down without too many problems, Alexander progressed to scrambled egg on toast. After that the pace quickened and the gastronomical choice widened.

As Alexander was immobile, the regular blood tests had to be carried out at home and the samples sent on to the laboratory. For this we enlisted the help of my GP. Not only was his surgery nearby, but as an advocate of natural healing methods, he could advise us about household remedies. To control the painful mouth sores, he prescribed a course of Ayurvedic tablets. Whether the ancient Indian medicine did the trick or not remains unclear, but the ulcers certainly disappeared, never to return.

But my favourite was the poultice recipe. Mix a handful of fenugreek seed powder with some warm water to form a brown paste and spread thickly onto a clean tea towel. Wrap carefully around the tumour and cover with a bathroom towel to keep in the warmth. Leave in place for at least an hour.

Within minutes, every room in the house smelt like a Tandoori restaurant! But as Alexander found it peculiarly soothing and it also satisfied my deep-seated need to do something *practical*, we continued with the curry cure and enjoyed its relaxing effect.

And for me there was the doctor's offer to pop into the surgery every fortnight for a chat and check-up – I could not afford to be ill as well.

The stitches along the biopsy incision had long since been removed and the wound had healed well. But now I had to come to grips with the Hickmann. On the oncological ward the medical staff routinely sent me out to the empty corridor to wait while they changed the dressing. Once outside though, I had begun to ponder. Who would do it at home? Presumably I would. And I had no inkling of how to remove the sterile plaster, clean the open wound, flush the line or prevent an infection.

Back into the room. Standing my ground against the team of doctors and nurses in white coats – 'Please stay *outside*!' – cost me considerable courage and precious energy, but it did result in my being given a crash course in Hickmann care.

Now I had to prove that I could do it on my own. I hadn't really understood why Alexander always felt so nervous until I tried peeling off the see-through plaster without accidentally tugging the line under it that protruded straight from an open hole in his chest. Then I was terrified too.

Partly to convince ourselves that we could play a trick on the germs, but mostly to boost our confidence, I shut the door of his tiny room. Then I arranged the utensils on a tray; sterile gloves, bottles of brown disinfectant, disinfectant sprays, a supply of the large, sterile transparent dressings, rolls of sticking plaster, scissors, cotton wool swabs and a rubbish bag which I tied to the end of the bed.

Alexander, who used to drive his severely handicapped patients single-handedly in a mini-bus from Hamburg to Denmark, had voted in a general election and shaved every day, lay helplessly on his back, fluffy bootees on his feet, waiting for his mother to change his dressing, like a baby with a nappy.

He needed assistance to take off his T-shirt. His wasted muscles tensed with apprehension. After washing my hands and applying liberal doses of disinfectant, I then donned the gloves and began easing off the previous day's sticking plaster. Alexander might have lost the hair on his head, but he had retained his few chest hairs. They clung stubbornly to the plaster. Alexander winced.

At last, the plaster came away. I could start cleaning. It was a tricky business. Very carefully, I dabbed at the sticky residue and checked for signs of inflammation around the line. Then a squirt with disinfectant. At this point Alexander always insisted I put on a fresh pair of sterile gloves before fumbling with the peel-off back of the new dressing. Trying to position it without any creases or air bubbles was an art of its own. Finally, I rolled up the 30 cm or so of line, like a coil of white liquorice, and secured it on his chest with strips of ordinary brown sticking plaster. Only then could we relax.

With time we developed a certain competence. Very gradually, I lost the fear of making a mistake, hurting my patient or overlooking an infection. Alexander seemed less cramped. We savoured the intimacy, the mutual trust, the cosy chats. In the end, he would allow only me and one nurse to touch his Hickmann – an honour indeed.

To facilitate communications with the outside and inside world, Wolfgang invested in a cordless phone for Alexander. With this system he could make both external and internal calls and Alexander was secure in the knowledge that he could always reach us no matter where we were in the house.

He missed his computer. He had only just purchased it with his hard-earned money and now it was sitting safely but idly in Chris and Irene's attic in England. Wolfgang provided technical relief by setting up an older model but with internet access, on a swivel arm next to the bed.

Once he started to feel brighter, Alexander vent much of his pent-up aggression on computer games. Ben was in his element. For a while he even forgot his own mysterious aches and pains that cropped up sporadically in his knees; the fear of contracting cancer too sent shivers down his spine. The two lads linked computers and spent many happy hours in amicable contests. Occasionally, Ben would hop into bed with his older brother ('Careful! My leg!') and the two of them would hammer away at the keyboard to accompanying jubilant shrieks of 'Got you!' or 'I won!' When our doctor came, he had to clamber over a maze of cables and wires in order to get near his patient. But he remained unruffled. It really didn't matter, he told us. And anyway in a small room the soul cannot get lost.

For Natalie, who showed understandably little interest in eliminating aliens for hours on end, the situation remained unsatisfactory. During the last traumatic weeks, our attention had centred more or less exclusively around her brother, shaking the foundations of her own world yet again.

She withdrew into her bedroom. Clothes, sodden towels and school exercise books lay strewn ankle-deep on the floor. Her plants dried out and the fish in the aquarium suffered an involuntary diet. In the evenings she went out and came home later and later. Once she disappeared completely for three days. We had no idea where she was. The increased stress of the final year at grammar school did nothing to alleviate the situation either.

Stew on Wednesdays, on icy cold days apples baked in the wood-burning stove in the living room, a plaid and a cushion on the sofa, a chat after school – everybody longed for some residual security and comfort.

And then the household. Alexander had arrived with one suitcase of clothes containing long trousers and thick pullovers, hardly suitable attire for a hospital bed. I kitted him out with new T-shirts and loose boxer shorts that would slide easily over his twisted and swollen knee.

Washing and ironing took top priority over the rest of the house-work. Nevertheless, bed linen, towels, trousers and shirts trailed out of the washing basket, the unironed clothes were stacked in heaps, every third light bulb had gone on strike and the whole house looked vaguely neglected and gloomy.

Had it been different before? Probably not. But now every little chore required Herculean effort. I dreamt of crowds of well-wishers who would miraculously turn up at the front door, brandishing dusters and armed with a large cake. They would brush away my feeble protestations – 'So kind of you, but it really wasn't necessary, you know' – along with the whole mess. Within a short space of time, everything would gleam and we would all sit down, tired but cheerful, for coffee and cake. If I had had the courage to ask for help of this kind, I'm sure people would have obliged. But I was too embarrassed to say anything. So nothing changed.

But I did find the strength to contact the local branch of the Cancer Society, miles away on the other side of town. I wanted to know whether any self-help groups existed. The friendly lady there knew only of a local Children's Cancer Organization (for children up to age 15) or a group for women with breast cancer. Adolescents and young adults – nothing doing, she said.

Then I remembered that the teenage daughter of an acquaintance had recently undergone treatment for cancer. I gave her a ring. She explained that she had tried unsuccessfully to start a self-help group for parents of teenagers; only one person had signed up. But with me there were three of us. We met at regular intervals, somewhere in town in a café or pub so that we had a glimpse of the outside world. And how we enjoyed being served for a change!

From the other mothers, I heard for the first time that we could apply for a disabled pass for Alexander. We swapped notes on everything: medical questions, tips on how to deal with our older children's tantrums and moods, recommended reading material; we shared our own worries, fears and tears. Fellow sufferers speak the same language.

Almost without realizing it, we had all slipped into a Siamese plural.

'We've already had an infection, a temperature of 40 degrees, just imagine, so we had to be admitted to hospital. They gave us antibiotics, and the blood tests, let me tell you, were never-ending. Till the leucos went up and we could go home – I'm not joking, we were at the end of our wits.'

It was as though we had melted with our children. Indeed, we did spend the greater part of our time in hospital with them. Even more reason then to create a counter-balance. Short phases of inactivity, swimming, sauna, cycling along the Danube, watching nature programmes on television – all that helped me renew my flagging energy.

The flood of 'get well' cards had dried up and were replaced by bills, a seemingly endless stream of manila envelopes with the word 'Liquidation' printed on the letterhead. Every day, Wolfgang devoted up to an hour with filling in forms, rectifying mistakes, adding his signature, filing and sending things back. His daily exercise consisted of walking or cycling into town to deliver the day's forms to the two insurance offices and then going to the bank.

Alexander did not interfere. The financial aspect he saw as parental responsibility. Our fiercely independent son actually welcomed having parents who dealt with bills and administration work!

But to be fair, he had enough on his plate already. He could not keep up with the assignments for university. We pinned all our hopes on his being able to go back for the summer term. In the evenings Alexander wrote in his journal. Nobody was allowed to read it. It was his private world, often the only place left for him to retreat to.

Only one more week and he had to go back to hospital. Our conversations took a new turn, revolved increasingly around shoes, legs and the amputation that hung over us, like the sword of Damocles.

So far, Alexander had declared that he would rather die than lose his leg. Now the time had come to start facing reality.

Alexander nagged me about his down-at-heel shoes. The protracted limping around in England had worn down the soles on one side. He begged me – *please*, Mum – to have them repaired. Much too late did I understand how much this errand meant to him psychologically, denoting as it did that he would soon require both shoes. I promised to see to it. But I didn't. Partly because I could see no reason for hurry (he couldn't walk anyway) and partly because it was beginning to dawn on me that in a few weeks the surgeon would have no choice but to amputate and Alexander no choice but to agree.

I wondered how the mushroom man – Alexander's visualization of his tumour – was faring. Could he feel any changes, I asked him?

Alexander shrugged his shoulders.

'Not really. Unless you count the fact that his smile has faded slightly and he's looking just a tad fuzzy round the edges. But he's still leaning hard on that spade and that's what makes everything so unbearable.'

In the last couple of days, the intensity of his pain had reached a new climax. We learned to interrupt our conversations until the worst had past. A call to the hospital gave us permission to increase the daily dose of painkillers a little. This new development did not bode well, we thought.

Yet at the same time, Alexander felt his frozen leg gaining in flexibility: he could actually move it a tiny bit and, albeit with considerable effort, succeeded in manoeuvring himself in and out of bed. Conflicting signals. What did it all mean?

Looking at Alexander's shoes collecting dust gave me an idea. A friend of ours had suffered from polio whilst a young man. He had survived with a matchstick-thin leg and a fair limp. If modern surgery could find a way to save Alexander's leg (which seemed highly unlikely), then the result would, I supposed, bear some semblance to Klaus's disability. Maybe a chat with somebody who had come to terms with his fate could be helpful? Alexander acquiesced.

The meeting turned out to be a direct hit. Alexander insisted on welcoming his visitor in the living room, propped up as comfortably as possible with piles of cushions on the sofa. Klaus had not seen him since the onset of his illness and he was visibly shocked at the sight of his deathly pale complexion and smooth scalp.

Cake – home-made! – and plenty of coffee broke the ice. Klaus launched into the story of how, as a young student at university, he had taken to his bed with a severe cold, then felt so poorly that he had phoned the doctor. The latter had admitted him to hospital immediately. When Klaus woke up the next morning, he could not move either of his legs. The following day, he could not move his arms either. Nobody could do anything except wait and hope.

Alexander listened, spellbound. He nodded.

'That's exactly what happens to patients with multiple sclerosis. Most of the patients at the home I worked at told me that if they had known what was going to happen, they would have killed themselves right at the start.'

Klaus ignored this remark. He continued with the revelation that the paralysis had stopped at that point, but that he had spent two months in hospital undergoing intensive physiotherapy and that, bit by bit, he had regained the control over his legs. First he sat in a wheelchair; then he walked on crutches. One day, a doctor had asked him why he was still hobbling around on sticks instead of standing on his own two legs.

'So I tried it. He was quite right, you know. I really could walk without them. To begin with, just a few steps. But then more and more. And as for this apology of a leg, well, it doesn't bother me at all any more. You get used to it,' he finished with a laugh.

A short discussion from man to man followed. Would a deformed leg have an adverse effect on relationships with the opposite sex? Klaus thought no, not necessarily. Alexander looked mightily relieved.

They finished with the Great Leg Competition. It was Klaus's idea. He suggested that they compare legs and the winner – the one with the puniest leg – would receive the last remaining piece of cake as a prize.

Laughing and with much theatrical drama, the two men revealed the exhibits. Klaus surveyed his own painfully thin and fragile-looking leg and then studied Alexander's critically. If calf-size were the main criterion, then Alexander had already lost, he mused.

'But I suppose we should consider the whole leg, from top to bottom. And you are quite clearly the winner there. I admit defeat. Your leg is puny all the way down and your thigh quite superbly wasted away. And I must say, that scar you have running down the side of your knee adds a certain aesthetic quality. The cake is clearly yours! Congratulations!'

Before he left us, limping off down the garden path, Klaus had two further suggestions to make. He offered to ask a young friend who had lost a leg in an accident to visit Alexander and chat to him. That would cover worst case scenario Number Two. Alexander agreed, but repeated that he had no intention of parting with his leg. Klaus also thought he could borrow a wheelchair for us, an offer that I accepted enthusiastically, but ultimately to no avail. It stood for a fortnight in the hall, unused. Alexander preferred to stay at home rather than admit in public to being handicapped.

Before I went to bed, I caught Alexander trying to walk to the bathroom, propelling himself along the walls without his crutches. He was frowning with the effort.

'I want to know if I can walk on my own two feet. Maybe I've grown used to crutches too and have to learn to do without them,' he explained.

Three more days. Alexander's friend Philipp came to visit. The two of them holed themselves up in his tiny room, talking, discussing and laughing until Alexander fell asleep with exhaustion. I invested the time so saved in additional gastronomical activity. Not only did Philipp enjoy a healthy appetite himself, but he was expert at coaxing Alexander to eat as well. Every piece of toast was worth its weight in gold.

The penultimate evening at home. Alexander chose to have a film and feast session, with pizza delivered from his favourite restaurant eaten on the sofa while watching a film. We balanced trays on our knees, sat in a circle around the television and followed the video of his choice. Alexander laughed a lot. 'Let's do it like this every time,' he decided.

The following morning Philipp took his leave, promising to come again after the operation.

Hospital. Bad vibes waited for Alexander. We discussed the best way to dispel them.

'I want to hear the truth. Even if it's not nice. But then I can adjust. I'll have to make that clear and I believe the staff will be understanding. We just need to talk it over together and then it will work out.'

I packed Alexander's bag ready for hospital and ordered an ambulance for 7.30 in the morning. We both attempted to prepare ourselves for the chemotherapy. The next round would decide whether he would lose his leg or not.

6

A New Leg

Whether on foot or by bicycle, the quickest way to the hospital led over Rilke's bridge. No poet's corner, this narrow footbridge, perched above the deafening roar of the motorway, acted as a link between the hospital that had become a home and the home that had become a hospital.

Up the road, past the old people's home, over the bridge, a glance down into the chasm and already we were treading hospital ground. It didn't take ten minutes. Unless, of course, we wanted to dawdle, play for time, delay the inevitable for a little longer.

Because as soon as we had arrived, events moved ahead at full speed, leaving no time for reflection. Making decisions, taking action, hoping against hope that we had chosen the right course, hoping we hadn't hurt each other – that's what our daily routine looked like.

Alexander had once again taken up occupancy of his horizontal prison in the little single room. Before the chemotherapy could transform him into a heap of misery, he wanted to resolve two issues. First of all, he sought the reconciliatory conversation with the staff to clear the air.

The second point was of a more tactical nature. Of course Alexander understood that at that stage of the proceedings no doctor could prophesy the fate of his leg. But that was exactly why he had thought up a new strategy. If he asked the medics about the theoretical criteria for an amputation, then he would be in a better position, he hoped, to gauge his own chances. At the same time, he continued to insist mechanically that he would rather die than lose his leg. The problem was, which doctor should he approach?

Systematically, he worked his way through the list of doctors, shortlisting two or three. We talked about who might give him the 'better' advice. But that was not really the issue at stake. Deep in his heart, Alexander was searching for the partner who would promise him limb-salvation surgery.

In the end, he opted for Dr P. Alexander respected her matter-of-factness and, as she had been on holiday during the bottle episode, she had not lost face with him. But I made him give me his word that he would accept whatever answer he received from her with no further ifs and buts.

He lay back on the bed and breathed deeply. Now that the matter was settled, he could relax. Not even the news that the doctors wanted a new MRI scan done quickly could ruffle him. One of the hospital porters fetched him and his bed. I made use of the opportunity to do some shopping and cook lunch in peace.

When I returned in the early afternoon, Alexander was seething with rage. Apparently, the porter had delivered him punctually to the radiology department, where the receptionist had said they weren't quite ready and please to wait outside. Whereupon Alexander had been unceremoniously parked on his own in the dark, cold and draughty corridor, without crutches, without a bell, without a urine bottle – for four hours.

And as if that were not enough, when his turn finally came and the staff moved him from the bed to a stretcher, they handled his fragile leg so roughly that he screamed in agony.

Hours later he was still spluttering with indignation. He was anguished and frightened. Never again, he swore, would he allow anyone to leave him unattended anywhere, under any circumstances. I had to give him my word that I would accompany him on all future expeditions. Another new area of expertise for me to learn. Navigating the recalcitrant bed together with all the swaying infusion bottles safely through the corridors required practice and not a little physical effort.

The door opened and in trooped the senior doctors with the latest scans.

What did they reveal? The consultants were at loggerheads. Whether the tumour had shrunk or grown larger could not be divined with any certainty from the images.

And the pain? Almost unbearable, Alexander told them. It was high time that they switched to morphine tablets. The World Health Organization (WHO), the doctor explained to us, recommends a three-tiered treatment plan for patients with chronic pain. Stage One effectively contains most tumour patients' pain. Only those with severe symptoms require the higher stages.

When prescribed correctly, morphine does not cause addiction, confusion or even respiratory depression. We also learnt that the tablets work on a slow-release mechanism, developing their effect over a period of 8 to 12 hours. For that reason Alexander needed to build up the appropriate level first and then continue to take the tablets regularly. Swallowing morphine tablets when it takes your fancy, the doctor was careful to point out, is not only useless as far as pain management is concerned, but downright dangerous.

So we were clear on this point. But why had the pain returned with such a vengeance? What was happening inside Alexander's leg? How much bone had been destroyed?

Dr P popped in. She was blithely oblivious to Alexander's plans for her. Casually, he asked her what she made of the MRI pictures. Not much, she admitted honestly. After all, she was not a radiologist specialist. But if he liked, she could offer him her own ideas on the subject. Could she see his leg for a moment?

Alexander whipped back the covers to reveal a distorted and wasted limb. She inspected it from close quarters. How far could he lift it if she supported him with her hand? Alexander shook his head.

'Not far at all. But more than I could two weeks ago.'

'And bending? Is that any easier?'

'I don't really know. It hurts so much I try not to move it. But I can get down the stairs at home now.'

'Can you try it with me now?'

He hesitated. She looked at him and said gently, 'I promise I won't drop it.'

Slowly and with great care, she eased the poor leg up and bent the knee joint a little. It went surprisingly well. Did it seem more or less swollen? Was I just imagining things or had it really shrunk?

Dr P had an answer ready. In her opinion the increased pain resulted from tissue dying off. The dead and not yet decomposed cells were piling up, which in turn was leading to a localized increased pressure. Alexander was impressed – it all sounded very convincing.

And now the 64-dollar question. As though the idea had just occurred to him, Alexander asked innocently how a surgeon would – quite theoretically of course – set about establishing the extent of the damage.

The doctor's face gave nothing away as she launched into a lecture. Legs, so we discovered, can be divided into five compartments. Each part consists, of course, of the respective muscles, nerves, veins and so on. Depending on the degree of damage, a compartment can be saved or lost. As a rule of thumb, amputation occurs when four of the five – or sometimes just three – are irretrievably damaged.

At least, I think that's what she said. I had stopped listening. In my mind's eye I was dividing Alexander's leg into virtual lines, numbering them from one to five, then wiping out numbers one, three and five and trying to visualize the result. A very thin leg, I supposed.

Alexander, however, had listened intently. The doctor was standing at the foot of his bed. He looked straight into her eyes.

'Based on the information you have so far, what would you say: is there any chance that my leg won't be amputated? After all, I do feel rather *attached* to it, you know.'

She swallowed hard. Her hands gripped the bed rail so tightly that her knuckles turned white. A deathly hush fell on the room. But she held his questioning gaze.

'No,' she said, gently but firmly. 'You will have to come to terms with the fact that in three or four weeks you'll have only one leg.'

She was brave. Yet it was the only way to do it; knowing the facts reduces pressure, uncertainty increases it. She patted his shoulder and told him she had to go. He nodded silently and watched her shut the door behind her. I felt for his hand under the cover. There was nothing to say. He had promised to accept the verdict.

The chemotherapy was beginning to take its toll. He felt sick and dizzy. Everything was so triste.

On the way home, I made a detour into the town centre. To buy new boxer shorts. I chose the longest ones I could find. Long enough to cover the stump.

If anybody had thought to ask me which was the worst day, I would have said, without a shade of hesitation, Thursday, 20 February.

The day started off on the wrong foot with the arrival of the morning mail consisting of several hospital bills amounting to a five-figure number. Doctors' fees not included.

It continued in the wrong direction when I reached oncology an hour later. Alexander lay in bed, drained of colour. On the way to the X-ray department, somebody had handed him a file marked 'strictly confidential' to hand over to the radiologist. Naturally, Alexander had opened it immediately. Amongst the documents there, he had come across a report on the latest images. But here it stated quite clearly, according to Alexander, that the tumour had grown and now measured nine by seven centimetres.

Alexander's voice grew louder as he talked. Tears ran down his cheeks. He felt betrayed, not taken seriously. Why was he submitting to all this torture anyway? Apart from making him puke and pee, it obviously was having no effect whatsoever. I did not know what to say. There seemed no getting past the fact that the tumour was huge, dwarfed only by the size of the question mark over his fate.

Alexander needed to pass water again. I left the room to wait outside. I spent a lot of time in the lightless, generally deserted corridor. Every now and then a door opened somewhere and I would catch a fleeting glance of skeletal figures, bald heads and big, questioning eyes.

But today was different. From the room next door came commotion. A nurse jammed the door open wide. Minutes later with the help of a colleague she pushed out a bed.

It was covered with white sheets from top to bottom. Underneath, the unmistakable contours of a human body. I knew people died here. Only until then, I hadn't actually seen it with my own eyes, had been able to repress the thought. 'Do you get used to it?' I wondered.

I watched how they disposed of the body, the personal possessions, a life. And suddenly I knew: I did not want my son to die in hospital, another anonymous statistic. If it came to that – but of course it wouldn't – then I wanted him at home, secure with his family, where we could accompany him to a dignified end. Did he want it too?

Alexander called for me. I went back in to the room. He was exhausted and pale. Skin and bones under the white sheet.

'I don't want you to die in hospital. If that's the way it's going to end, then I would want to take you home.'

Alexander turned to look at me. A smile flickered over his face.

'That's what I want, too. Promise me, please promise me, that you won't leave me in hospital to die?'

I promised.

Lunchtime at home. Wolfgang was unusually subdued and quiet. He didn't feel well. Nothing serious, just a sore throat and a slight temperature. He'd just pop in to the doctor's for a check-up.

As the other members of the family were busy, I took over the afternoon shift with Alexander in hospital. He had reached the stage now where he no longer wanted to talk, have the curtains open, eat or drink. Apathetically, he lay in bed, waiting for the next bout of stomach-wrenching vomiting. Simply watching him was hell.

I consoled myself with the thought of spending a pleasant evening at the theatre with a girlfriend. After such a terrible day, I was looking forward to the treat very much indeed. I washed Alexander's face, emptied the slop bowls, fetched new ones, stroked his cold forehead and the sickness took no end. Not until he became quieter through sheer fatigue, and thought he might doze for a while, did I dare leave him.

In the kitchen I found a note from Wolfgang. The doctor had diagnosed a feverish cold and written him off sick for a week. He was at the chemist's picking up his prescription. Fine. I would just have to shoulder his shifts in hospital too. The main thing was not to infect Alexander.

I glanced at the clock. Just enough time to shower, change and grab a bite to eat before leaving for the theatre. But I never reached the bathroom. The phone rang. Police. Something's happened to Wolfgang or Natty, I thought. The policeman had to repeat twice that he was talking about Ben before I understood. A small offence, he said. Please come immediately to the police station.

The bumpy bike ride over the cobblestones shook endless feelings of guilt up to the surface. I hadn't paid enough attention to the needs of my younger son and this was the bill, a cry for help, an 'I'm here too' appeal. What should I do? How should I react?

I found the police station, introduced myself as the mother of the boy in custody – not a proud moment – and followed the officer to a room at the back. Ben was sitting on a chair, his face swollen with tears. When he caught sight of me, he broke into sobs.

The policeman read us the riot act. He spoke with a firm but friendly voice and looked at us meaningfully. The boy can't help it, I longed to tell him. Soon someone's going to chop off his brother's leg and probably he will die and we are all at the end of our wits and I can't take any more. But not a word came out. Instead, I signed for my son obediently on the dotted line.

On the way home, we agreed on a fitting punishment: a week's house arrest and extra chores. Ben sighed with relief. I made a last mad dash for the theatre.

There was no time for explanations. We ran up the steps and sat down just seconds before the curtain rose for the first act of Tchaikovsky's *Eugene Onegin*.

Even more, then, to talk about in the interval, which at 40 minutes seemed more than generous. Finally the bell summoned us back inside, where a nervous director was waiting for us, microphone in his hand. Unfortunately, the stage mechanics had broken down, he apologized. All three parts had jammed hopelessly, with bizarre consequences, he warned us, for both actors and audience.

So they had. The last scene required the presence of the whole cast. Some were standing on a raised surface in the foreground, others could just peep over the sunk central section and the rest was huddled together on the half-elevated part at the back. Subdued laughter rippled through the audience. It was too comic for words. I laughed until I cried, which is what I'd actually been wanting to do the whole, long, dreadful day.

When I walked into Alexander's room the following morning, it was to witness the by now familiar scene of a pile of bones with a skull protruding from the bed covers, a room dark and silent apart from the monotonous droning of the infusion pump, the bowls at the side of the bed overflowing with vomit. At least the pain had eased somewhat.

I made myself comfortable. Under the warmth of the blanket we held hands. Occasionally Alexander twitched involuntarily. From time to time someone tiptoed into the room to check the infusion and urine bottle. The ever-cheery cleaner lady peeped in. She'd come back later at a more opportune moment, she whispered. Doctors came and went. They, too, were subdued and monosyllabic.

Alexander breathed imperceptibly. Sometimes I dozed off until a noise startled me. Sometimes I felt confused. Was I sitting next to my mother at her death bed or my son? Without hair, they looked uncannily alike.

Another round of sickness announced itself, leaving Alexander completely drained. He slumped back on the pillows, temples pulsating wildly and breathing hard. Only once did he speak.

'How can a human being be so sick, Mum?'

Then he lapsed back into his twilight world.

Alexander weakened by the hour. Without my help he could no longer muster enough strength to sit up and vomit. Wave after wave of sickness overcame him, although his stomach had nothing left to yield.

Another attack. This time it lasted even longer. He shivered with cold and weakness, fought for breath. I guided him back down into bed, washed his face and hands, warmed him up again, moved the bowl a little further away and sat down on my hard chair next to the bed. Somebody had half-opened the curtain. I glanced out of the window.

I couldn't believe what I saw. I looked again. But it was still there: a rainbow! The colours shimmered at the peak of its brilliance, sparkling with serenity and beauty and peace. A rainbow in February? It must be a sign.

I stroked Alexander's cold hand. Try and look out of the window, I told him. There's a rainbow and I think it's for you.

He twisted round painfully and together we watched the spectacle until the colours slowly faded and finally disappeared. He said nothing. But he seemed comforted and fell asleep peacefully. I walked home.

A week later the treatment block was over and Alexander convalescing at home when the call came. Dr P was on the phone; her voice trembled with excitement. The team had studied the latest MRI images, which had been taken shortly before Alexander's discharge. Now there was not a shade of doubt: the tumour had definitely shrunk! She had just spoken to the operating surgeon about it. It would not be easy, but he was confident he could operate – without having to amputate!

She reminded us that Alexander would lose untold muscles and nerves, a large section of the thigh bone and the whole of his knee joint, and that the endo-prosthetic replacement would restrict the movement of his leg. But what did we care? Alexander would still have two legs. That was all that mattered.

'Told you so,' Alexander commented on the surprising turn of events. 'I told you right from the start that I intend to survive with two legs. You should really stop making such a terrible fuss.'

As soon as we had gone, however, he rang up all his friends in great excitement and passed on the glad tidings. Klaus was informed that the young man with the artificial leg need not bother to call any more. Then he immersed himself in his list of 'Nice Things To Do When You Are Not Being Flattened By Chemotherapy', which by now ran to several pages.

Once the sickness had subsided, the race against time began. We had to build Alexander up in the short time before the operation and subsequent chemotherapy. Food in all shapes and sizes featured prominently in the attempt.

But not only for Alexander. Wolfgang's condition had not improved. For the last week, he had been bed-ridden with a high temperature, complaining of strange noises in his ears and difficulties in keeping his balance. The doctor diagnosed an infection of the brain stem and extended his sick leave by a further fortnight.

To reduce the danger of cross-infection, father and son avoided direct contact, staying within the confines of their rooms on different floors of the house. Natty, Ben and I took precautionary measures and wore mouth masks when in their company. They communicated with each other via the internal house phone, each person answering with his own personal code or 'ward' number, as we christened it.

'Hello, Ward 23 speaking. I've run out of tissues. Could you bring me some more please? Thanks.'

'Ward 21 here. I'm feeling a bit peckish. Any chance of something to eat?'

'Ward 23 again. I've just been on the phone to Ward 21. Listen, I'm quite hungry too. Can I have an English breakfast with loads of baked beans, two fried eggs, four sausages, five slices of toast and a cup of hot chocolate? Ward 21 would like the same.'

I had my work cut out, running backwards and forwards, up and down the stairs. Still, it was preferable to being in hospital. At least we were all united under our own roof.

Alexander made progress. The pain subsided suddenly and when a friend came to stay for a few days, the two young men could even sit outside on the balcony in the March sun and take little walks with the crutches.

When we attended the appointment in hospital with Dr P and the operating surgeon to discuss the details, we were able, for the first time, to do without an ambulance. Alexander sat with his leg stretched out on the back seat of our mini-van and I drove us both over to the clinic.

Alexander was already aware that the endo-prosthesis would be firmly screwed into place at each end of the remaining bone. What worried him most was the extent of the resulting disability. The surgeon thought Alexander would be able to walk – eventually – but not run, and warned him that even then he might need walking aids. I wished I'd paid more attention to my physics lessons at school. It sounded as though Alexander's new leg would manifest properties similar to those of nut-crackers, only with the difference that he would not be able to bend it more than 90 degrees. That ruled out cycling, but might allow rowing.

Alexander pulled a face. The surgeon regarded him pensively and pointed out dryly that he could amputate the leg in 45 seconds. Would he prefer that? It would be much easier, run a lower risk of infection and, well, artificial limbs perform wonders nowadays.

Alexander rejected the offer with thanks and signed the consent form for an endo-prosthetic replacement. 'How do you make sure you are operating on the correct leg?' he asked casually. The surgeon spluttered and said he never mixed legs up. At home again, we looked through the files we had been given. Alexander's pictures were in the envelope, but also a set of X-rays showing the thigh of an unknown woman. We tried to keep calm.

The last evening before the next round of treatment, we celebrated with the now traditional pizza and video. Wolfgang had to miss out. Eating while wearing a mouth protector verges on the impossible. Father and son had not met face to face for the last two weeks. But there was no alternative. We cracked endless jokes about surgeons and operations and laughed nervously.

Natty and Ben left for school early next morning. I packed Alexander's bag, cut his toenails, cuddled him and comforted him. We delayed our departure for as long as possible. By early evening, we could not put off the evil moment any longer. I drove him back to the hospital in the van. The familiar smells, sights and sounds. Could I have taken him back to have his leg amputated?

On his crutches, but standing upright, he walked back into oncology. The nurse on duty was taken by surprise. She hadn't realized he was so tall. But the pleasure remained short lived. Soon he was back to a horizontal position, surrounded by infusions, urine bottles and blood samples. Still time for one last chat. I asked about the mushroom man.

'Gone. He went all fuzzy at the edges and then vanished. He's gone.'

No, he wasn't frightened. This was the third operation now and he knew what to expect. Was there anything else worrying him, anything else he wanted to discuss before I went? Yes, there was just a little thing. What? Tell me. I braced myself for what was coming. What would happen, Alexander wanted to know, if he needed to go to the loo after the operation; he wouldn't be able to walk. I thought he would be fitted out with an urinary catheter. Oh, right. A combination of relief and disgust.

Time to go. A last embrace with the bundle of skin and bones. A last glance at the delicately shaped head, fine nose, brown eyes, the wasted leg and twisted knee. He kissed me on the cheek.

The next time I saw my son, he was lying in the intensive care unit. During the four-and-a-half hour long operation he had lost a lot of blood, Dr P told me. Everything is fine, though, she assured me. If I wanted to, I could pay him a visit – she had seen him looking prettier, she said – and she would be glad to accompany me. Of course I wanted to see him. And I was immensely grateful that she went with me. Suddenly I realized just how bone-tired I felt. For a few minutes she took the burden away from me.

I trotted along beside her through endless corridors while she explained that Alexander was still unconscious and attached to 17 machines including a respirator. Behind the glass entrance doors was a small hallway. In front of us stood a shelf with caps, gloves and gowns. We put them on. On the left, a waiting room. A woman was pacing up and down, twisting and untwisting her hands. All around us monitors flickered. There. A reception desk. Behind it I could just make out three glassed-off rooms that appeared to contain corpses. One of them was Alexander.

With a white towel wrapped round his naked head like a turban, his deathly pale face and peacefully closed eyes and a tube in his mouth, I hardly recognized him.

He was a human spaghetti junction complete with contraflow. Tubes, infusions, machines and bleeping monitors everywhere. They didn't bother me much. What suddenly did bother me greatly was the duvet.

I simply had to do it. Very gingerly, I pulled it back. Yes! Two legs and the ten most charming little toes ever seen! We had won the first round. Now matters could only get better.

7

Mixed Outlook

The serrated edge of the saw, shining and lethal, drew nearer and nearer. It danced up and down, flashing eerily in the bluish light. Scattered around on the floor lay its previous victims: legs, in all shapes and sizes. Small ones and fat ones, shapely ones and deformed ones. Most of them had been neatly severed from the torso; only a few had bloody, jagged edges. All of them had drilling holes. In the background, I could hear a hum swelling to a whining shriek – the sound of a chainsaw slicing through tree trunks.

Squatting together in a corner were the mushroom men. They had crawled out of the amputated legs and were sitting there, lifeless, shadowy, strangely translucent. But one or two were still active, digging furiously with their spades and planting their spores in the earth.

A bodiless arm holding a saw swished past my face and moved resolutely towards the next leg. It was Alexander's. No, no! Not his leg! Stop! Leave him alone! You've got the wrong X-ray pictures. It's all a mistake…

I woke up drenched with sweat. More than a couple of minutes passed before I realized I had dreamt badly and that nobody was trying to chop off my son's leg. Now that the threat of the last months had suddenly dissipated, the bottled-up fear sought release in black nightmares. For three nights in a row, the saw terrorized my dreams. Then peace returned. How traumatic must it have been then for Alexander?

After 36 hours in intensive care, the doctors transferred him to the surgical ward. The nurse told me he was in the last room at the end of the corridor. I would have found it anyway – I could hear Alexander's screams a mile away.

I wished fervently that he would stop before I went in. I did not know how to react. And there was no handbook with instructions. Slowly it dawned on me that, although we had won the first round, many more trials and tribulations were in store for us. Would it never end? I wanted to run away, let somebody else sort it all out. I wanted to be normal again, have normal, everyday problems, like losing the house key or missing the bus. But there was nobody else there.

I opened the door. Standing next to Alexander's bed stood a nurse, hands on hips, appealing to her patient to concentrate on his breathing. He screamed in reply. I was speechless. I had never seen Alexander in such a state before.

The nurse summed up the situation. To banish the risk of infection from any pre-operative germs that might have been lurking in the old sheet and duvet cover that had come with him from oncology, they had just changed the bed linen. Naturally the nurses had been forced to lift Alexander up a tiny bit. The pain would be only temporary, she assured me before beating a quick retreat and leaving me alone with him.

I walked over to Alexander, looking for an undamaged part of his body to hold and comfort. He was attached to three lines running through a junction and connected with the Hickmann. Tubes protruded from both hands, his fingers were yellow and black from bruising. Standing on the bedside table a pain pump with a morphine cassette. Wrapped round his ears and nose an oxygen mask. Between his hip and foot seven drainage tubes, held securely in place with sticking plaster to the fresh bed linen. They trailed lazily down to the floor where their bloody contents slid into seven glass bottles. I opted for a yellow hand. Alexander screamed and screamed.

When eventually he was able to talk, he still spluttered with rage and pain. Did they want to kill him here with their sheets? Why hadn't they changed the linen with the pre-operative germs while he was lying in intensive care? I couldn't think why either. So I listened until the venom was spent and he was nothing but a sobbing, tear-stained, helpless lump of pain, and dozed off through sheer fatigue.

He was quiet now, his breathing regular. I sat down on the hard chair next to the bed and surveyed the scene. Little red globules huddled together on the inside of the tubes at the edge of the bed and peered anxiously into the abyss below. They jiggled and danced and shivered. Eventually, one would summon up courage and take the plunge, slithering down the tube at breakneck speed, only to stop abruptly and for no apparent reason half-way down before – seemingly defying the laws of gravity – sliding repentantly back up to rejoin its more apprehensive siblings. Only after several such abortive attempts did a globule of blood succeed in completing the journey to the underworld.

Those were the good minutes when I could watch this spectacle. Most of the time I spent listening to Alexander. Everything bubbled angrily out of him: how he had woken up in intensive care and thought he would suffocate; how cross he was with me because I had omitted to take a photo of him there. Only when the breakthrough pain had him pressing the morphine pump were there any gaps in the conversation. And anyway, what did it look like now, his leg?

That's what I wanted to know as well. Again and again I needed to reassure myself that it really and truly still existed. At the same time, I was scared to look at it. Gingerly, I teased the coverlet back. From top to bottom, the leg was covered in bandages and, apart from a slight hollow in the hip area, everything seemed surprisingly normal.

I didn't realize that a post-operative swelling was providing the familiar curves until the following day when, at Alexander's behest, I had another look. To encourage the healing process and let the air circulate, the nurse had removed the bandages and wedged the poor wobbly leg to prevent it from slipping sideways. To sum up: a clean wound measuring 58 cm – I had thoughtfully brought a tape measure with me – held together with no less than 60 stitches. A real work of art on a leg that now sported the roundness of a cricket bat. Alexander was clearly relieved.

Other matters, however, were less satisfactory. After a quick break from the hospital and Alexander to do the shopping and feed bed-ridden Wolfgang, I came back to hear raised voices emanating from Alexander's room. The door burst open and four hot and flustered male nurses stomped out into the corridor.

I hardly dared go in. In my absence Alexander's anger had replenished itself and was about to burst. He let fly a torrent of abuse. The nurses, he snarled, had come in with the intention of heaving him, the drips, the morphine pump and his seven drainage bottles into a wheelchair and taking him for a walk. He had refused. Categorically refused. They had had a good talk to him, waxed lyrical about the advantages of early movement and at the same time had attempted to lift him out of bed against his will. Alexander had defended himself by shrieking in agony.

'It's *my* leg. *I'll* decide whether it's good for me or not. If they dare touch me again, I'll scream and scream until a doctor comes. I can't stand any more of this. Why are they doing this to me? Why?'

And he sobbed and cried, his nerves completely shattered. Once again, he had lost control over his body, lost his independence, his need for privacy and, to a large extent, his right to decide for himself. His sense of dignity was wounded to the bone.

Alexander swore revenge. Hunger strike! Not a morsel would pass his lips, he vowed, until he could pat the letter of discharge in his pocket. This was not quite as heroic as it sounded. He had no appetite anyway and was already being drip-fed with vitamins and calories. But it was the psychological element that counted. Apart from half an Easter bunny's ear which he had nibbled at shortly beforehand, he kept his word.

But matters didn't stop there. In the long run, I was the obvious target for his pent-up wrath. Alexander had backache and, despite the nurses' administrations, pressure points were developing on his elbows and heels. Moreover, his leg kept slipping in the wedge and, full of panic at the thought of the ensuing pain, he jabbed away at the morphine pump.

It was my job to try and realign his leg. Just touching it made him cry out in pain and me shake with nervousness.

'More to the left. Not *that* far. Stop! You're killing me. Can't you even do that right?' When I had finally found an acceptable position, anchored his leg with a pillow and sat down, it slipped again and I had to start from the beginning. No matter how hard I tried, everything I did was wrong, useless or hurt him terribly.

Another test of my patience was the piped oxygen supply. He needed more of it; no, not *that* much, for heaven's sake. Or less of it, or it should be more bubbly, or less bubbly, faster, no slower. I was in constant motion, trying to fine-tune the control dial, but nothing ever suited him.

The third day after the operation represented a further negative highlight. On his morning round, the surgeon told Alexander that a sample from the tumour had been sent to a specialist laboratory in Vienna ('Mum, if I die, you won't know where to put a gravestone for me – there are bits of me all over the place') and then, without any prior warning, tugged at one of the drainage tubes and pulled it out. Alexander screamed and screamed and screamed.

'When exactly does it hurt?' another doctor asked him a little later.

'Whenever a consultant or doctor steps within a one-metre radius of my bed,' Alexander retorted nastily, giving himself an extra shot just to prove the point.

But that sentiment wasn't quite correct. Every evening after coming off duty on oncology, Dr P walked over to the other side of the hospital to visit Alexander on the surgical ward and keep him company for a while. Sometimes she took my place with him. For her visits, he had no need of a pre-emptive dose of morphine. And she had a surprise in store for him: now that the tumour had been removed, he technically no longer counted as a cancer patient. He liked that idea very much.

Only when the pain had started to recede could Alexander cope with a visit from his brother and sister. Natty gave her brother two little chocolate Easter eggs and for a moment he was tempted to call off his hunger strike. In the end, his pride came first and he left them untouched on the table.

It was the hour of the physiotherapists. Alexander had to blow into a plastic tube with a ball so he wouldn't catch pneumonia, twiddle his toes for exercise and pull away at a strip of green rubber ribbon. After a week or so, the loathsome urinal catheter disappeared and the last drainage tubes came out. Because he wasn't eating, Alexander received daily high-calorie infusions along with the stream of antibiotics. Thick as clotted cream, they frequently jammed the Hickmann line and occasionally the blocked junction had to be broken open with force. Alexander carved the words 'torture ward' maliciously into a cushion pad.

And we waited. Waited for tests, waited for the results of the tests, waited for a free bed on oncology, waited for the next chemotherapy.

It seemed an eternity before the surgeon appeared with the pathology results. He took up position at the foot of the bed. Alexander watched him expectantly.

'You are a very lucky young man. The tumour was completely dead – necrotic, we call it – the surrounding area was not infiltrated and the bone marrow showed no signs of malignant cells. You could hardly hope for a better prognosis.'

Alexander grinned.

'Well, it looks as though I really have won the first leg. Now all I have to do is survive.'

On the first day of spring, ten days after his arrival for surgery, Alexander was moved back to oncology. He managed to take a conciliatory farewell from the staff.

Being back on the familiar ward felt – heavenly. Alexander's room was ready waiting for him, as too the next round of chemotherapy.

Dr P marched in, a bottle of bright liquid in her hand. She wore protective latex gloves while setting up the infusion. She asked whether Alexander understood why he needed further treatment. He thought so. He knew that, in all probability, the tumour had formed nasty little cancerous cells in the blood stream which nobody could see or detect, and which were just waiting for half a chance to attach themselves to something that secondary tumours find attractive, lungs for instance, or the brain. Post-operative chemotherapy offered the only chance to render the invisible beasts harmless.

The doctor nodded in agreement. Then the next blow. The unpleasant job of handing Alexander the rest of the protocol timetable had fallen to her. For the period after the operation, patients were allocated to different groups depending on their individual risk factor which determined the length and type of chemotherapy to be used. Like 80 per cent of all cases, Alexander had been assigned to the standard risk group and that meant a grand total of 18 rounds of chemo and a further 20 weeks of treatment from now. Twenty weeks!

Without saying a word, she looked at Alexander. He was fighting back the tears, all the ebullience of the previous day wiped away.

'Well, that's it then. I can't keep up with university, can't go back to England. It was all for nothing,' he stated resignedly.

Our concerted efforts to build up Alexander's hopes that he would be able to continue his studies in early summer, and be reunited with his friends in England, were destroyed once and for all.

For the second time, our trust in the medical staff was severely tested. Of course it is a shock to hear you will be hospitalized for eight months, but it is even more demoralizing to be told four months, only to discover then that this isn't true. Again, there was no security, nothing to hold on to.

This unexpected turn of events placed me in a difficult position as well, as I could no longer cancel the study trip to England I had booked and organized single-handedly for July without incurring severe financial penalties. Now I would have to travel and leave Alexander behind in hospital.

Chemotherapy number seven. Unhurriedly it dripped out of the bottle and paved its way through Alexander's veins.

After two days of treatment, Alexander announced to our great relief that he wanted to learn how to walk again. No sooner said than done. An apparatus which we nicknamed the 'leg machine' because at the time we did not know its real name, namely a CPM or Continuous Passive Motion Machine, appeared in the room, and mechanically and slowly bent Alexander's artificial knee joint to a predetermined angle for a few minutes each day. Two human therapists complemented this activity with breathing exercises. Then came the day when Alexander, dizzy and befuddled though he was, could sit for a few seconds with their help on the edge of the bed.

After that it was only a question of time before he could pull himself up on the pulpit frame and stand on his own two legs! Shaking and wobbling, beads of sweat on his forehead and supported by the two physiotherapists, he drew himself up to his full height. It only lasted a minute or so and then the strain became too great and he had to give up. But it was a considerable triumph, both physical and mental, and nothing motivates like success.

On the very next day he took his first faltering steps. Three people had to support him; two on either side and a third to trundle the infusion stand along behind him. From the door I watched as he dragged his sewn-together leg behind him, his face knotted with effort and concentration, his tall, gaunt frame silhouetted in the light of the window at the end of the corridor. Members of staff stood still, clapped encouragement and egged him on. Behind his back I cried tears of joy.

Final preparations for Alexander's homecoming were also in full swing. Dr S made no attempt to conceal his good humour ('You should switch from computer science to medicine, Alexander, you know so much they could easily let you off the first year!'), and promised faithfully that he could go home on Saturday. He seemed so sincere that we decided to believe him.

But first the 60 stitches had to come out. After removing about 20 with the pincers, both Dr S and Alexander wearied of the job. They decided to leave the rest to our GP.

The last bottle of saline solution had nearly run through. Alexander was like a boat in a lock, waiting impatiently for the water level to drop so he could be freed. Without consulting anybody, he increased the speed of the infusion. Nobody dared say anything. His eyes wandered restlessly between the bottle above him and the clock in front of him. The alarm! 'Finished!' he called jubilantly and the waiting ambulance men lifted him carefully onto the stretcher and at last, at last, drove him home.

It was the beginning of a new era. The whole family felt hollowed out and shattered, so it was fortunate indeed that Alexander's discharge coincided with the two-week Easter school holidays.

Alexander abandoned his hunger strike and, once the post-chemotherapy sickness had worn off, embarked on solid foods for the first time in many weeks.

Ben gladly accepted an invitation to go away for a week with friends. A break from our never-ending nightmare would do him good, we all agreed. Natty came and went, withdrawn and unpredictable. Both siblings had received little attention. Wolfgang was convalescing slowly after four weeks in bed and, as there seemed to be no further risk of infection, we relaxed the visiting regulations; father and son were able to meet face to face again.

The next-door neighbours dropped in with a pot of yellow-gold daffodils, Klaus visited bearing a basket overflowing with fruit, Easter cards from Britain clogged up the letter box and, by Easter Sunday, Alexander could even eat some of the cooked lunch.

Routinely we went about the home care. As our own GP was on holiday, his stand-in dealt with the regular blood tests and the remaining stitches. The latter caused us considerable headaches. When lying down, Alexander could not move his leg of his own accord and, as the bed stood in the corner, the operation scar faced the wall. It was dark and cramped in the tiny room. How was the doctor to get anywhere near the 40 remaining stitches? We could think of no other solution but for both the doctor and me to clamber into bed with Alexander, rather like three men in a boat. I held a flashlight in place while the doctor bent over the little black threads.

Alexander still relied on his daily morphine tablets, but found he could gradually reduce the daily dose as the doctor had prescribed and without any secondary effects, until finally he no longer needed them. Another step in the right direction.

With the help of a charming and vivacious physiotherapist who came to our house every day, Alexander made more progress concerning his mobility and independence. She monitored the angle at which the CPM we had hired ran – 20 degrees to start with – showed him how to pull his trousers over his legs, taught him simple exercises to do in bed, chatted to him easily and assiduously massaged the skin over the wound which was sticking to his knee.

After four or five days, he was ready to take the staircase in his stride. Our concerted efforts were required here. A fall could damage or even snap the residual bone around the prosthesis and an amputation would be the certain consequence.

We formed a human chain on the staircase in front of Alexander in order of size: first the physiotherapist, then me and Wolfgang bringing up the rear. I had visions of us all tumbling down the stairs like dominoes, but although Alexander faltered frequently and six hands shot out to catch him each time, we all kept our balance.

When we asked him what his leg felt like, Alexander informed us that, contrary to general opinion, titanium seemed to be a strangely soft metal, bordering on the consistency of Angel's Delight, in fact. Persuading his toes, calf, knee and thigh to move simultaneously and in unison required all his powers of concentration. Yet within three days he could navigate the stairs on his own, providing somebody walked in front of him to catch him if needs be.

That was how matters stood when Alexander had to return to hospital. The consultants called for a new MRI scan and, when the pictures were available, Alexander asked Dr P to be allowed to admire his new leg. No problem. Alexander let us help him into a wheelchair and we pushed him and the obligatory drip stand along to the doctor's room.

Before switching on the monitor, Dr P reminded us of the details. A section of bone measuring about 25 cm had been removed from his left thigh, his own knee joint was missing and another section of bone from the calf had also gone, she said. The surgeon had hollowed out the remaining bone at each end, hammered in the endo-prosthetic replacement and secured it in position with strategically placed horizontal bolts. It all sounded perfectly familiar, nothing we didn't already know.

One click and there it was, the new leg! Just as she had explained to us and a very neat job too. But Alexander froze with horror. He stared at the screen in disbelief.

'This is crazy! There's nothing left of my leg! A miniature stump at each end and everything else consists of a metal rod! It isn't a leg at all. It's an artificial limb, camouflaged with my skin. He should have amputated it after all. It would have been better than this fake here!'

I hadn't foreseen this outburst. It had simply not occurred to me that Alexander could mentally reject his new limb.

He hated it. For him it was nothing but a foreign body that he could not accept. Or at least, not at the beginning. Over the coming days he grieved – at last – for the loss of his real leg. He could not shake off the feeling that he had suffered a kind of back-handed amputation. Quite subjectively, he felt tricked and deceived. Only gradually did he grasp the bitter truth: he would never again have two healthy legs. From now onwards he was physically disabled.

But he was not going to accept that without a fight. There would be no 90-degree restriction for him. *His* leg would be much more flexible, achieve more, we would see.

According to the protocol, he faced a three-week block of treatment next. It came as a pleasant surprise then to hear that he might come home for two days between doses. Everything ran smoothly. Alexander had given up his resistance to cortisone and had to admit grudgingly that the pills really did reduce the gruelling nausea to a bearable level.

Freed from this scourge, Alexander felt hungry and developed a voracious appetite. On a typical day he wolfed down no less than eight meals. As hospital food reminded him of chemo and disinfectant, I cooked for him at home, packed the meal into containers and reassembled and reheated it on the ward. This elicited much interest among the younger members of staff who expressed their willingness to help out if Alexander couldn't manage everything!

The days started off with a generous cooked breakfast. A little later Alexander felt like a snack, a big bowl of muesli with fruit perhaps, or cornflakes. He downed litres of banana milkshake. At lunchtime, I cooked a three-course meal and Alexander often devoured two helpings.

In the afternoon he had cake. Large slices oozing with calories and enough cream to make your veins coagulate just looking at it. And as a little something to keep him going, mounds of toasted sandwiches.

Naturally he was ravenous by teatime, so another three-course meal could hardly be counted as a luxury. Early evening served to remind him just how peckish he felt and that he really could do with some more toast or semolina pudding or whatever, and of course we sympathized when, at ten at night, he was nearly fainting of starvation and demanded pizza. For the odd moments in between, he kept a liberal stock of sweets, chocolate bars and fruit on the bedside table.

We watched Alexander filling out, kilo by kilo, in front of our eyes. Hospital staff and friends all breathed sighs of relief and said how wonderful, how pleased we must be.

And it was lovely. For a while. But then it turned into drudgery. I found it harder and harder to cope with the never-ending shopping trips, the sheer volume of cooking and the washing-up, all in addition to the gruelling hospital shifts and teaching my classes. Nor was Alexander the only patient in the family who needed to be fattened up; Wolfgang had lost weight too after his illness and, at 16, Ben was always hungry.

Alexander admitted himself to being a bottomless pit. Even when, in my despair, I started to buy frozen foods and take-aways, I still couldn't keep up with the increased demand. The situation was threatening to get out of control. And nobody understood. More and more, my frustration centred on Alexander.

One day it erupted. Since the early morning I had been cooking, making sandwiches and mixing milkshakes non-stop. By eleven at night, I was on the brink of collapse. But just then Alexander complained petulantly that he had hardly had a bite to eat for hours and how about a baguette with cheese, tomatoes, lettuce and…

I lost my temper. 'That's enough. I'm not bringing you any more food today and I don't care if you have cancer or die tomorrow. I'm going to bed!'

There. I'd said it and I didn't regret a syllable. I stormed off, threw myself onto the bed and wept.

The next morning I went to the doctor's. Jittery nerves and fatigue, he said. A calming infusion would do the trick. Within minutes, the tables had turned; now I was the patient. People asked *me* how I was feeling, checked *my* drip. I could be crotchety if I wanted because it was *my* nerves that looked as though they had just come out of a mincer. After an hour there, I felt more relaxed and composed and could afford to sympathize again with my starving and now completely hairless son.

So far Alexander's eyebrows and eyelashes had withstood the unrelenting chemical warfare successfully. But now they too had capitulated. From one day to the next they disappeared, transforming Alexander's facial features dramatically and rendering his eyes itchy and helpless against invasions by foreign bodies. During the night, his eyes gummed together and in the morning I had to bathe them with warm water before he could prise open his eyelids.

We needed something to brighten us up. But what? The answer came when I glanced at the calendar and realized that the coming week represented the fifteenth in the treatment plan. Half-time! That called for a celebration. And I had an idea.

8

Better Days

If one single object symbolized the misery of the last months, then it would be the infusion pump. It whined and hummed in the background, monitored and dispensed the chemotherapy. So why not make it the centrepiece of a half-time party? An infusion cake, gentle on the stomach and therefore easily digestible, must have a therapeutic effect!

With the aid of a photo featuring the details, I explained to the baker what I had in mind. The correct spelling of 'half-time' caused a lot of head scratching, but in the end we came to an amicable agreement, also concerning the colour scheme and proportions.

Meanwhile, the real, inedible pump next to Alexander's hospital bed was running true to form: Alexander battled with severe sickness stemming from the exquisitely pretty, but equally lethal, liquid – cisplatin – in the bottle.

His condition at the end of the chemo required the presence of paramedics and an ambulance to take him home. Although Alexander claimed to be fit enough to tackle the stairs on his own, the men linked their arms together to form an 'Angel's Seat', and carried him upstairs; Alexander suffered his helplessness with angelic patience.

Adapting to the roller-coaster track of progress and setback posed us all with a considerable challenge. After the latest spell in hospital, Alexander yearned for privacy, autonomy and a hot bath. The wound on his leg had healed sufficiently to allow contact with water, so he just needed to make sure that the Hickmann didn't get wet. So far so good. Whatever he did, we impressed on our son, he should not lock the bathroom door from the inside. He promised. Wolfgang and I had to do some shopping for the planned family celebration. The siblings stayed to 'look after' their brother.

No sooner had we rounded the corner in the car than Alexander felt like a new person and decided to treat himself to a relaxing bath straight away. And because he felt so much better and confident, he locked the bathroom door on the inside. Once submerged in the soapy water, however, he suffered an attack of weakness. He tried to get out of the tub, but his stiff leg, poor circulation and the high sides prevented him. He lost his balance and slipped to the floor.

Natty and Ben heard the dull thud and rushed to help. But of course, they could not open the door. Several anxious minutes passed before Alexander managed to drag himself to the lock and turn the key, allowing his brother and sister to rescue him from his plight and carry him back to bed.

All three of them were badly shocked. As a family we walked a tight-rope: if we were over-protective towards our son and brother, we ran the risk of stifling him. Too lax, and he could do himself a serious injury.

On the whole, I trusted Alexander's own gut feeling. Normally he was the best judge of what he could and could not do. But this episode taught us that he, too, could slip up.

The day of the party. Long before grandparents, aunts, uncle and cousin arrived, there was a ring at the doorbell and the baker's van delivered an enormous cardboard box.

One thing became clear immediately – the cake's creator had obviously never set eyes on a real infusion machine in his life! The cake was a flatter version of its electronic model and consisted of a sponge base, decorated more or less in line with the original, with pieces of dyed marzipan. On the left, a small box with the number 250 – the speed of the infusion – in a shocking pink. Right at the bottom, a second box closely resembling a marshmallow and sporting the words 'Half Time', and on the right the on/off switch. Everything lay superimposed on a sickly green background.

It was the right-hand side that caused general hilarity. Mounted on a sludge-brown slice sat a pasty object that resembled, well, a severed penis. Goodness only knows what it was supposed to be.

What should we do? Remove the object of offence or trust in Alexander's sense of humour? In the end, we didn't interfere. After all, it did consist of solid marzipan, a much relished treat.

The guests began to arrive. They hadn't seen Alexander since the beginning of his illness. We had grown used to the physical and psychological changes, had moved along with them, but for the visitors everything was new. As a result, the conversation with Alexander moved along jerkily. What do you say to somebody who has no hair, no eyelashes and no eyebrows? How do you breach the gulf between the sick and the healthy?

After lunch, we announced the surprise. Alexander we instructed to sit on the sofa and shut his eyes while Wolfgang wheeled in the cake, looking more authentic now we had attached it to a real infusion bottle donated by the ward.

But when we said he could open his eyes now and look, Alexander couldn't. In the short time of waiting, they had gummed together again and I had to wipe them with warm, wet cotton-wool buds before he could see anything again. He stared at the strange apparition before him.

'What the devil is that supposed to be?'

We shuffled uncomfortably and coughed. The pale marzipan phallus gleamed up at us from the table. I stammered out an explanation. Slowly a smile spread over Alexander's face.

'Well, what are we waiting for? Let's eat it!' he grinned.

And in an act of the highest symbolism, we consumed Alexander's pump cake with the greatest of pleasure.

Outside, in the normal world, spring had arrived. The juicy green young leaves on the trees supplied a hint of colour after the long, dark winter months. The air was fragrant with apple blossom. Even our neglected strip of garden awoke to new life and fought to survive; the cultivated plants struggled against being throttled to death by the treacherous ground-elder. Just like in hospital. In the corridor, someone had hung up a cartoon depicting a stork in the process of swallowing a frog. But by cleverly wrapping its long hind legs in a stranglehold round the stork's neck, the frog was not making it easy for its attacker. 'Never give up!' read the caption underneath.

Like nature, we too were seized with a desire to catch up, grow and develop. Alexander was making huge leaps of progress. He continued to put on weight and could bend his leg so far that it was no problem for him any more to sit in our van. What unheard of depths of freedom! Now we could dispense with home visits by the physiotherapist and GP. We had broken through the vicious circle of hospital–home–hospital.

To sit behind the steering wheel again, no longer to be dependent on us, to move freely – these were Alexander's dearest wishes. The car became *the* symbol of freedom. But as yet he still had only restricted control over his leg. What would happen if he couldn't react quickly enough in a traffic situation? A test drive on a private road would provide some of the answers, we thought. Alexander beamed.

As his strength returned, Alexander devoted himself to reading literature. Until his powers of concentration – impaired by the chemo – improved, he stuck to short stories. But bit by bit, he progressed to longer and more detailed books until eventually he could pleasurably work his way through the French and Russian classics – food for his soul.

He should spend as much time in the fresh air as possible. At least, that's what I thought. I tried to encourage him to take walks. It was a laborious task, as the crutch handles rubbed against the palms of his hands. We experimented successfully with padded biker's gloves to relieve the pressure and prevent the angry red blisters.

Every day we walked a few steps further. How uneven the pavements seemed! Each little road had a menacingly high kerb, the distance between the benches nothing less than a marathon course. Sometimes I felt an unreasonable anger welling up inside me towards this towering son of mine, who crawled along next to me like a toddler with his mother. Passers-by and car drivers turned back to stare brazenly at the bald young man on sticks. Alexander didn't let it irritate him. 'They can stare if they want to,' he said. 'What the hell.'

Whenever we could, we tried to get as far as the 'Wave', a metal sculpture on the riverbank. Under the crest of its steely wave, two people could find shelter in a semi-upright position. Cocooned with its sun-warmed frame, Alexander soon forgot about his aching back and tired legs. We rested and watched the water on the Danube flashing in the sunlight. And as if we were holding a shell to our ears, we could hear the far-off roar of ocean waves.

How horribly hard, then, to take leave of such golden moments, to return to hospital, to be subjected over and over again to the debilitating treatment, independency and passivity. Alexander grew increasingly impatient.

One of the first improvements he introduced became known as the 'urine trick'. If he collected the output of 24 hours in a jug at home immediately prior to the chemotherapy, he found he could save himself one whole useless day in hospital, the only disadvantage being that our mode of arrival then mutated into a circus act. As we rarely had the good fortune to find a parking space nearby, we had to walk a long way to the ward. While Alexander waded along manfully as though on stilts, I struggled along next to him, juggling his suitcase and at least a litre of smelly pee swishing around in the lidless clinic container!

But then this particular body fluid posed problems all round. After he had fallen asleep one night, still clutching his overflowing urine bottle and had woken up drenched, Alexander lost his patience. He demanded a urinary catheter *now*, please. Oncology didn't stock them, so someone was sent to fetch one from the geriatric ward. Back he came with a kit that simply did not accommodate the needs of a young adult male.

The correct size had to be ordered, but once it eventually arrived, it revolutionized Alexander's nightlife. Without disturbing his sleep, the night nurses could still monitor his lethal distillery, documenting his progress on a sheet of paper under the headings 'input' and 'output'.

Something else was fermenting in the emotional vat. Alexander caught us unawares with the bitter accusation that we had forced him to undergo treatment against his will. What's more, he swore that, in the event of a relapse, he would never agree to any further chemotherapy. He would rather die.

A passing mood, we believed, and we attempted to cope with the situation by being patient and understanding. Sympathetic counselling from a third party would have been appropriate at this juncture. But there was nothing available and so the dispute smouldered away.

After yet another round of accusations and allegations, I got hot under the collar. Without saying a word, I rang for a nurse. Alexander looked confused. When she came, I asked her to remove all the lines and infusions because Alexander had decided to stop all treatment. She threw him a questioning glance.

Now it was up to him. I didn't care any more. I felt much too hurt and burnt out. We waited for him to reply. In a very small voice he said, 'No. No, I don't want that. Don't unhook me. It's a misunderstanding. I shall complete the course.'

He glared fiercely at us. 'But I shall never agree to any more chemotherapy after that. Never. Is that clear?'

He really did mean it. Nor could you mess him around about his discharge times. He had tired of waiting obediently for the doctors' final word. Alexander knew perfectly well which blood results had to be attained and when before he could safely be sent home.

If anyone so much as hinted that his estimated minute of discharge might prove unrealistic, he flared up and obstinately repeated his ultimatum. To keep the peace, the doctors increasingly relented. Alexander cut more and more corners.

We settled down to a new routine of three days in hospital and four days at home. The weekends at home passed quickly, but in hospital they seemed interminable. On warm days in May, Alexander would lie in his little room in the clinic and spend hours watching the swallows as they darted back and forth to their nests under the eaves. On one side of the wall, new life hung suspended in a pocket of mud. On the other side, old life hung at the end of an infusion bottle.

After chemotherapy and flushing, he walked out of the ward on his own two legs. With the aid of crutches, but upright. There were no hitches, no setbacks, no unforeseen difficulties. Nobody bothered to wear mouth protectors any more. Visitors no longer had to prove a clean bill of health before being admitted into our house. Of course we kept an eye on the leuco count, but there was never any reason for concern.

We became more relaxed. And bolder. We treated ourselves to a family breakfast at the pavement café in front of our erstwhile castle home, we meandered through the bookshops, took ourselves off for a picnic at a nearby lake, spent an evening at a cabaret and, best of all, went to the cinema.

Alexander was beyond caring whether people might infect him. All he wanted to do was watch a film in the cinema. So little to ask. With a wry sense of humour, he chose to see *The English Patient*, although its length caused him a certain amount of physical distress. Not being able to bend his knee properly meant that the whole weight of his leg pivoted relentlessly on his heel. But Alexander was willing to put up with the throbbing ache in exchange for passing a few hours in the company of healthy, fellow humans.

Contact with other patients in hospital increased too. After months of isolation in his single room, Alexander now found himself sharing with one, two or, occasionally, three others, generally older men who invariably robbed their room-mates, already subjected to constant decibel torture from the motorway outside the window, of the last vestige of sleep by snoring loudly all night and turning their radios up by day.

When their wives and daughters and sons and grandchildren came to visit, they quickly filled the room to its limits, and Alexander, still chained to the bed and with a constant need to pass water, quite often found himself in an embarrassing situation.

But that was nothing compared to the burden of being confronted with other people's tragedies. The first time Alexander witnessed – unwillingly – a death sentence passed on a room-mate, the experience rocked him and he could not hold back the tears. It wasn't so much the awful diagnosis itself that troubled him, but rather the seemingly blunt manner of delivery.

We tossed this problem back and forth and also discussed it occasionally with the staff. One day, a notice appeared on the door of the doctors' room. 'Please do not disturb. I'm thinking. Dr S,' it read. We made inquiries and learnt that the ward doctor was doing some calculations. The result? Under the prevailing working conditions, he worked out, the doctors could devote an average of one minute a day to each patient. Nevertheless, the hospital authorities were planning to cut back further still on jobs. Hardly surprising, then, that some things went by the way.

'We are so sorry. We can't do any more for you.' We watched how patients and their families struggled with their fate. Generally it followed the same pattern: the relatives would complain vociferously about the hospital and the doctors, claim to know of a better therapy available in another clinic and assure the patient that he most certainly was *not* going to die. Outside the room, in the corridor, they would burst into tears.

The patients, on the other hand, would appeal to Alexander not to tell their families that they knew they were dying, as they were afraid of causing their loved ones anguish and worry.

Only one young couple behaved differently. They made no secret of the fact that the man had no future and they thought long and carefully about how they might best spend the remaining time together. Sometimes they lay together in the bed next to Alexander, kissing and cuddling – and why not? Alexander had no objections.

One lovely spring day, I was standing alone with the young man at the window. Below us we could see the car park. Silently we watched the people rushing around and then suddenly he asked me what it was like out there, in the normal world, when you are not being eaten away by a brain tumour. I could find no answer. I hardly knew myself any more.

Alexander and I agreed that, should he ever be the terminal patient, he would want transparency, honesty and trust. No games, no play-acting, please, Mum.

Another change to our routine occurred with the arrival of a girl on the ward, just diagnosed with an osteosarcoma. Alexander lost his coveted status as the youngest patient, but gained the role of experienced adviser. An element of competition crept in as well, as Alexander was loath to appear wimpish! The two of them struck up a friendship, consolidated with visits to their respective rooms on the ward (or notes or phone calls if the risk of infection seemed too high), words of mutual encouragement and much laughter, all of which helped boost their morale and keep them in good spirits.

It all started quite harmlessly. When I came back from work one morning, Alexander was still lying apathetically in bed. Interrogation revealed that he had a slight temperature and a scratchy throat. He was irritable and tried to play it down. No wonder. It was his week at home. I put a call through to Dr P in hospital and described the symptoms.

She seemed unsurprised. She had been expecting a setback for some time, she said, because Alexander had been cutting too many corners considering he was still being bombarded with huge amounts of highly toxic medication. She asked if he wanted to come back to hospital. He'd rather die than do that, I suspected. So she decided we should call in the GP first.

Natty and Ben were anxious. I tried to reassure them that a course of antibiotics would soon have their brother back on his feet and an infection, well, that had been bound to happen sooner or later. They nodded silently.

I rang the surgery and arranged for a home visit. Only I couldn't wait for the GP to come, as I had an evening class to teach. Wolfgang was away for the week on a school trip, so Natty agreed to be in charge.

It seemed an eternity until the school gong went at 9 p.m. and I could go home. Natty updated me. Alexander was now running a dangerously high temperature, Ben was picking up a prescription for antibiotics at the chemist's and, according to the blood test the GP had taken, his leuco count had plummeted to 300 and we were to take Alexander back to hospital immediately.

Fortunately, he offered no resistance. He felt so awful, he had no strength to protest. Ben and I helped him into a tracksuit, and between us carried him down the stairs and bundled him into the van. At the entrance to the hospital, we grabbed a wheelchair and pushed him over to oncology where we were awaited. Not a word from Alexander.

Within minutes, he had taken up single occupancy of a double room. It was very late. Ben and I had to leave. On the way home, I was plagued with guilt about abandoning my son like this, but also about having recklessly endangered his health. If he were to die now, I would be partly to blame, I thought.

By the next morning, the crisis was under control with a course of penicillin for the infection and morphine for the painful sore throat. But even those few hours of being unwell had left their mark. The padding Alexander had built up in the last weeks seemed to be disintegrating in front of our very eyes. His throat hurt so much he wouldn't speak. Under the coverlet, I sought his hand. Such demonstrations of love had gone out of fashion recently; now they were back in demand.

After four days, he felt well enough to come home. But nothing was the same any more. The sense of – relative – security had vanished. We were all badly shaken at the revelation that there were no shortcuts and that, despite theoretically counting as an ex-cancer patient, Alexander's life still hung on a fine thread. No longer could we take our bearings from the timetable, because the next chemo had to be postponed by a week until Alexander had staged a complete recovery.

This setback took its toll. Alexander seemed subdued, demoralized, irritable. One day, the phone on his bedside table rang and the caller asked in an unnecessarily loud voice whether he was talking to Mr Schubert. 'No,' Alexander shouted back, 'this is Mozart here!' and slammed down the receiver.

The chemotherapy might not have destroyed his natural wit, but it was getting increasingly difficult to keep him appeased. Yes, we discussed literature. Yes, he showed interest in my preparations for the study trip. Yes, he had turned into an empathetic and often equal conversation partner. But after quarter of an hour at the longest he would say, 'I want out!'

I had to come up with some good ideas. On a sultry afternoon in early summer, Alexander threatened to discharge himself immediately, on his own responsibility. The first blood test had already met the necessary discharge criteria and he refused to understand why he should have to stay in hospital for another two hours. Every additional minute that he spent there counted. I suggested we disconnect the infusion ourselves – it was only the last bottle of saline solution – slip furtively out of the room, buy an ice cream at the kiosk in the entrance hall and take a walk outside. By then the last batch of results should be back and he could go home.

Alexander agreed reluctantly. The long corridor was deserted. Nobody noticed us creep along to the lift like burglars in the night. Miraculously it arrived promptly. Nobody inside. The doors had nearly closed when we heard hurried footsteps outside. They sprang open again and the senior consultant stepped inside.

He smiled at Alexander benignly. 'Well, young man. Going home, are we?' he asked. 'Yes,' said Alexander.

'No,' I said. We exchanged dark looks before Alexander relented. 'We're just going for some refreshment downstairs and then we'll be back.'

Alexander demolished the ice cream in no time at all and then remembered that he had actually just wanted to walk straight out of the hospital through the doors.

'Okay, let's do just that. Shall we take a look at the helipad?'

For months we had watched the red and yellow helicopters flying past the window, but we had never seen them land. As luck would have it, one flew in just after we had laboriously hobbled round the buildings. We sat on a wall, taking stock of how a team of men in bright red boiler suits extricated a body from a hole, scarcely larger than a coffin, lifted it on to a stretcher and then ran with it towards the emergency department.

Nothing more happened. Boring. We cast around for a new diversion and hit upon the bottle banks. A hospital worker was just emptying a bucketful of used infusion bottles. One after the other, he threw the glass on to the pile where they smashed noisily. Alexander made some rough calculations. Not counting the smaller ones, he reckoned he alone had used 800 one-litre bottles so far, enough to fill, or almost fill, one whole bank.

That afforded him a certain satisfaction. Could he have another ice cream, please? Then we sneaked back to the ward where staff were now searching for him in desperation. He showed no sign of repentance, but stuffed his discharge letter into his pocket and, as fast as his crutches would permit, beat a dignified retreat out of the hospital.

Puberty all over again. The more independence Alexander gained, the more demands he made on family and friends. He tested boundaries, redefined the parent–child relationship and grew up a second time. Duties, of course, were part and parcel of it. As soon as he was physically capable, I insisted that he carry his own plate into the kitchen. In order to keep one hand free to hold the plate, he had to hop on one leg and one crutch. But he didn't complain; he had matured beyond his years.

He had also learnt his lesson concerning infections. Shortly after I had dropped Alexander off for his physiotherapy one morning, a phone call came to tell me that he had collapsed and I should come immediately.

I rushed back to find a chalky Alexander and a physiotherapist blaming himself for his patient's condition.

We drove straight over to the hospital. The leuco count could not have been worse. Below 200. Alexander knew what that meant – solitary confinement. I left him alone in the room, drove home and cooked lunch. Wolfgang and Ben complained of sore throats too. Natty didn't come home at all.

In the afternoon, I returned to the ward. On Alexander's door I found a sign, warning visitors not to enter but to report to the nurses' station first. This had never happened before. Had things taken a turn for the worse? So as not to put my son at further risk, I had to disinfect my hands, squeeze my hair into a cap and don plastic shoes and sterile gloves. This time it took three days before he recovered from the infection and could be sent home.

Alexander was just trying to catch up on his sleep when the phone rang. Wolfgang's father had been rushed into intensive care in a hospital 70 miles away. Wolfgang jumped behind the steering wheel.

Later on in the evening, the phone rang a second time. But this time it was about Natty. She had been admitted to the emergency department of another hospital in our home town. The doctor on the end of the phone sounded earnest and menacing.

'She's swallowed something and overdone it. But we don't know what. If you don't tell me what she's taken, we might not be able to pull her through.'

9

Happiness

I f only I had known. Wolfgang returned in the late evening and had not even clambered out of the car when I broke the news to him that we would have to drive straight to the next hospital.

Natty was lying on a bed, still unconscious. She had been treated with an antidote and now everyone was hoping for the best. She was suffering from withdrawal symptoms. We stayed with her until the early hours of the morning. Slowly, her heart beat calmed down and the doctors could tell us the danger had passed. Somebody handed us a plastic bag containing her shoes, purse and other personal belongings.

We had come to the end of the road. For years we had struggled to keep our daughter at home and out of a psychiatric hospital. But now we had to admit defeat; we could no longer manage. Not Alexander *and* Natty. We just could not cope.

The following morning, Natty was transferred to a drug clinic from which she immediately discharged herself and then promptly disappeared, barefoot and with no money. The clinic did not notify us. Hours passed before we realized what had happened. All day we sent out search parties. To no avail. In the evening she came home of her own accord. We explained to her that we loved her very much, would always support her, but that we could no longer live together. Professional therapy in a drug clinic, that's what she needed. Natty agreed reluctantly.

We asked for another appointment with the same hospital, saying it was urgent. The doctor on duty leaned back in his armchair, stretched his legs out in front of him and kept his eyes firmly shut while I attempted to outline the progression of Natty's illness and explain our current state of emergency. The lack of eye contact made me feel very nervous. Sometimes I even had the impression that the doctor had fallen asleep.

Still with eyes closed, he stroked his chin.

'Could it be,' he mused, 'that you would like to park your daughter here for a while just because you are experiencing a few problems with your son?'

The accusation of parental guilt hung heavily in the air. But we could see no other solution. Natty desperately needed professional help and, whether at fault or not, we parents were not in a position to provide it. In the end, we all agreed she would be admitted to the closed ward.

If the clinic offered any kind of support for the relatives, we heard nothing about it. Just trying to make an appointment with a doctor seemed to verge on the impossible. We would willingly have cast about for something else, but we didn't know where to start, where to look. And anyway, we were too tired. So Natty stayed there, fashioning picture frames in the occupational therapy sessions, sticking shards of old mirrors onto the wall to form a mosaic and letting us feel her cold anger.

'There is an end, you know. It will be over soon,' said Dr P to me in English. That comforted me very much. She had sat down next to me as I waited on oncology for a bed for Alexander, waited for the results of his blood and urine tests, weight checks and cortisone tablets, and waited for the next round of chemotherapy. Waiting with no end.

The treatment dragged on and on. Why were we doing this anyway? How much longer could we bear it? Alexander said that it had become a way of life. He could barely remember what he had done before, let alone imagine this state of affairs would ever stop.

That's how it struck others near us too. The longer the treatment continued, the less sympathy it aroused. Once the threat of amputation had been banished in March, some people had drawn a mental line under the whole unpleasant affair and were genuinely astonished to hear that Alexander was still on the ward in July.

Alexander? Three members of the family were now in hospital needing visits. Our despair made us inventive. 'If you take over visits to hospitals A and B, then I'll go to hospital C. Tomorrow we can swap.'

Whenever possible, Alexander visited his sister, treating it as a matter of honour. Climbing the many steep stairs up to the third floor wore him out and he frequently had to stop for a rest. At the top, we had to ring the bell beside the locked, frosted glass door and wait for someone to open it. Inside a lamp flashed. That was the signal. A toddler, dummy in mouth, appeared on the other side of the glass. With outstretched arm, he strained unsuccessfully to insert his toy key into the lock. He lived there on the ward with his mother, behind bars. The mother–child unit had no spare capacity.

Then the security measures. Hand over our bags, take off our jackets. Staff carried out various spot checks ranging from a breathalyser to a urine sample produced under the watchful eyes of a nurse to prevent any manipulations. If you were clean, you could enter the ward. Then to Natty's room to try and engage her in a discussion. Often she gave us the cold shoulder, vented her anger on us. We had to be sure to leave punctually or else she would incur penalty points. And as we left, we heard the key turning in the lock behind us.

Yet another type of therapy lay in store for Alexander. Dr P had mentioned a rehabilitation programme and brought along with her someone from the hospital's social service department to Alexander's bedside. It was the first and last contact with a facility of which we knew nothing except that it broadcast frequent and loud announcements on the intercom system, inviting patients to forget their woes for an hour and try their hand at cross-stitching. The system placed too many hurdles between the patient and help; only if the head nurse considered the case worthy would she pass on the details to the social services, who in due course would contact her again, requesting her to tell the patient to call in personally at the office which, needless to say, was hidden away somewhere in the bowels of the hospital and only open for short periods on alternate days.

To begin with, Alexander had resisted the idea of rehabilitation with hands and feet, or what was left of them. For him, it simply spelled out more hospital, and he had had enough of that. Dr P tried to win him over with an analogy borrowed from the business world. His leg represented his capital, she told him. The more he invested in it, the higher his reward would be at the end. Because he was keen to drive the car, and that as painlessly as possible, Alexander gave in and promised to go to a specialist rehab clinic on completing the cancer protocol. But only for three weeks, instead of the standard four. He looked at us defiantly.

'I'm going to buy a car. That's what I want. In five years I might be riddled with metastases and die and not even have had the pleasure of owning my own car.'

That was how matters stood when I left with 24 of my language students for our 12-day study trip to England. I hated the thought of leaving Alexander and Natty behind in their respective hospitals. For months, I had not left the city boundary and I had severe misgivings about the whole thing. But the trip turned out to be a wonderful, shared experience. The weather was clement, the Victorian hotel cosy, the group interested and lively and the outings to the honey-coloured villages of the Cotswolds a welcome diversion from the sunless hospital corridors.

Amazing how much difference an absence of a few days can make. When I came back, I saw things with other eyes. Alexander, I realized now, could no longer be confused with a pipe cleaner – he had put on weight. A combination of physiotherapy and leaning on crutches had broadened his neck and shoulders, making him strong and muscular. The scar along his leg had healed up beautifully and was hardly noticeable. And his knee! He could bend it – just – to a 90-degree angle and even hold the position for a few seconds. Both the leg machine and the hired hospital bed were now superfluous and at last we could furnish his room at home normally. Within the house, Alexander could dispense with his crutches altogether.

But best of all – his hair was beginning to grow! As though it no longer cared about the murderous, chemical attacks, the fine, fluffy down grew in concentric circles on his naked head. Everybody wanted to touch and stroke. The psychological effect was enormous; having hair again signalled to the world that he was healthy again.

Two more rounds of chemotherapy to get through. Dr P came into the room with number 17 wedged under her arm, but instead of attaching the line, she sat down next to Alexander's bed and fiddled with the bottle. She had a surprising offer to make. Things were going so well, she said, that, if he wanted to, Alexander could forego the last two treatments, adding with a grin that it simply wasn't any *fun* any more. Alexander burst out laughing, but steadfastly refused. He was going to see the matter through to the bitter end. All 18 rounds, please, and no shortcuts.

So he stayed there in the room with two older men. It was hot during those summer days in late July. How to pass the time? We stared out of the window at high-rise flats, the television tower with its red warning lights and, at its feet, a group of pristine allotments and huts flanked by four flag poles. It looked vaguely like a medieval castle…

We let our imagination run riot, with Alexander taking the lead.

'The television tower is the inner keep where the princess in distress is being held captive. And the flats are the soldiers' quarters. They have to guard the prisoner. But whom do I see there? A knight. He's approaching the castle moat. Oh, it's the King's son, accompanied by his most faithful servants. Look, they are storming the castle walls!' (A wisp of smoke trailed over the ring of allotment huts.)

'They are fighting to the death! Shots are ringing out!' (The infusion machine was bleeping madly.) 'The prince is a hero, determined to rescue the damsel with no thought for his own safety.'

('That's daft. If he doesn't make sure he stays alive, he can't rescue the object of his desire, can he?' 'Oh goodness, don't be so pragmatic!')

'Yes! He has fought his way through to the innermost sanctuary where he finds his true love and rescues her from the hands of her captors. The townsfolk too are delighted to be freed from evil and celebrate for days with feasts and dancing. They hoist their flags from all the poles and everybody lives happily ever after.'

Well, that had been a bit of fun. And what did it all mean? Was Alexander the prisoner, or was he the valiant knight ready to die for his true love? He shrugged his shoulders and gave no answer.

Philipp delighted Alexander with another visit between chemotherapies and then it really came to the very last, final round.

It was cramped in the fully occupied three-bed room. Relentless too the summer heat. The August sun burnt through the slits of the lowered outer blinds, transforming the patients' pyjamas into striped prisoners' jackets and bathing the room in an eerie, yellowish glow. Sweat poured down everybody's faces.

A woman pushed open the grey door and walked in. She had come to visit her husband who was sitting on the bed, an oxygen mask coiled round his ears and nose. He gasped for breath. Nobody spoke. Idly, the woman picked up a leaflet from the table entitled 'Nutrition Guide for Tumour Patients'. For a while, she flicked through the pages. Suddenly she bent forward in excitement and, with hope in her voice, said, 'Darling. Listen to this. It says here that malt beer is highly recommendable for cancer patients. I'll buy you some. You never know, perhaps it will...' She didn't finish the sentence. The man with no air stared emptily at the floor. He didn't answer. Everybody in the room knew that he would die soon.

Dr H popped in for a quick chat. She said that Alexander had been very brave and commanded her respect. Tears sprang to Alexander's eyes. Then she reminded him that the Hickmann would have to be removed in a small operation the following week.

Dr S squeezed Alexander's hand and said that everything had gone well, thank goodness. Now we'd have to hope that no metastases appeared. Only after ten cancer-free years could one speak of having beaten the osteosarcoma.

An hour later and Wolfgang and Ben joined us. Only Natty was not there and we missed her terribly. For Alexander, I had prepared a surprise. With the aid of cocktail sticks, I had fixed a number of chocolate cake bars together to form the word 'END' and decorated them with 18 candles, one for each chemotherapy. Tensely, we all scrutinized the last infusion bottle and counted first the minutes and then the seconds until the final drop disappeared into the tube. Ben ceremoniously lit the lights. Wolfgang whipped the empty bottle off the stand, pushed some sparklers through the neck and put a match to them as well. Everything burned and sizzled and glowed.

'I am never, ever, going to have chemotherapy again,' Alexander sobbed. 'Never. I would rather die than go through that again.'

He wanted to go home. The room-mates watched in silence as I packed his things in the bag.

'He's so young,' muttered the man with the oxygen tube. Tears trickled down his cheeks. 'I'm old, I've lived; it doesn't matter. But him – he's only a lad.'

Nurses and cleaners lined the corridor as we walked out, Alexander on crutches, but upright and triumphant. They wished him all the best and hoped he would never come back, told him they would miss him and hugged him goodbye. Then they wiped his name off the board with a damp cloth.

Minutes later Alexander was walking hurriedly up the path in our front garden, past the reception committee of red and white balloons bearing the inscription 'Love you' and which insisted on hanging upside down on the string like a multi-coloured colony of bats. He stepped over the red-crêpe carpet adorning the steps, glanced quickly at the bouquet of 18 red roses on the table in the living room, and even rushed past the kitchen fragrant with the smell of his favourite dinner cooking in the oven, and headed straight for the bathroom; his poor bladder was at bursting point.

Long awaited events invariably turn out to be anticlimaxes and the end of the treatment was no exception. Our daily life carried on much as before. As always, the bills continued to flood our letter box every day. Hidden under his T-shirt, Alexander's Hickmann still required fresh dressings. Every morning, Alexander drove himself to the physiotherapist and did his workout in the gym. Twice a week, he walked over to the GP for blood tests and waited for the results.

Not to mention the final examination in hospital. Alexander's ability to hear high-frequency sounds had been slightly affected, but his heart and kidneys had – miraculously – escaped damage from the highly toxic chemotherapy.

After two months in hospital, Wolfgang's father had recovered enough to be discharged. Only Natty was still in the clinic and we continued to visit her once a week.

School holidays! Ben found himself a summer job and Wolfgang and I enjoyed the – relative – peace in the house. Time to go for walks, drink coffee, read the newspaper, visit friends. Just nice, simple, ordinary things.

As I peeled off the plaster for the last time, I asked Alexander if he would miss the Hickmann. He snorted. No, hardly, he said. Unlike me, he felt no emotional ties to his lifeline. I was the one who would miss the intimate little chats, his closeness and his trust. But our son wanted to stand on his own two feet again, and that was just fine.

Going back to oncology, an overnight bag under our arms, evoked conflicting feelings. On the one hand, we still belonged there. On the other hand, we didn't. By the afternoon, the Hickmann had been relegated to the history books. After the operation, hospital rules stipulated that Alexander should stay in overnight and remain under observation, but Dr P simply did not have the heart to refuse his pleas to let him out the same day. He promised to come back without delay should any problems occur. Then it was time to say a last farewell to the hospital and the oncology ward and its staff and patients.

Alexander had barely enough time to test drive the second-hand car with sunroof that we had bought for him on his instructions, before he had to park it in the garage and let us drive him to the rehabilitation clinic in the Bavarian Forest. Nestled high up on the mountainside, the magnificent building enjoyed sweeping views of the valley.

We left Alexander behind in the stillness and solitude and stayed away so he could settle down. Only once did we visit; he needed to recuperate from us as well as the chemotherapy. When we did see him, he made us laugh telling us about his football feats. As an endo-prosthetic replacement patient, he explained, he was at a serious disadvantage compared to the chaps with proper artificial legs because if you kicked them on their iron shins they just grinned, whereas even the slightest brush against his sensitive, half-real leg caused him to writhe in agony and lose the ball!

I wanted to get away. Anywhere. As long as it was warm and sunny. Ben felt the same. We booked a last-minute flight and ended up in Bulgaria at the Black Sea. For a whole wonderful week, we splashed and swam in the shallow water, walked for hours along the beach, enjoyed each other's company. Ben let off steam with windsurfing.

Alexander spent his twenty-first birthday without us in the clinic; he was discharged two days later on his brother's birthday. After four months in hospital, Natty could also at last come out. No more hospitals! We celebrated with a gourmet meal at a restaurant, staged a barbecue with the young family next door and invited the self-help group over for coffee and cake.

Then the next changes to our family life. For Natty, we rented a room in a flat. Optimistic and reconciliatory, she planned to go back to school and complete her education.

England and university of course were waiting for Alexander. His state of health did not yet permit him to drive his car such a long way on his own, so very sensibly he took his place in the queue for a flight to Birmingham at the airport, new black rucksack on his back, leaning on the turquoise crutches, suddenly embarrassed that it was all over and we would have to part.

From the other side of the glass panel, we waved to him. The security guard asked him to place his crutches on the belt and another man routinely ran the metal detector over his body. Right leg – nothing. But the titanium-filled left leg set off such a piercing alarm that everybody turned round and stared. A red-faced Alexander attempted to prove his innocence. Eventually the man shrugged his shoulders and let him through. We all breathed a sigh of relief. One last time Alexander turned round, smiled shyly, waved and – was gone.

Life without him was strange. I slept badly, often waking up in the middle of the night, dreaming about infusions or legs or mushrooms. During the day, I was paralysed with chronic fatigue. I spent every spare moment sleeping. Making a list of the day's tasks, reminding myself to pick up Alexander's medicine, arranging appointments for his physiotherapy, buying him a cake – it took a while before I remembered that it had stopped, the end had really come.

I even missed the hospital. I missed the little chats, the daily routine and the sense of relative security it brought. People in the normal world couldn't understand why I didn't throw myself heart and soul into learning Russian, digging up the garden, reading Shakespeare's collected works or go mountain biking for a couple of weeks. Everything was fine now, wasn't it? How could I describe this immobilizing exhaustion and the fear of a possible relapse?

Alexander also had to find his way laboriously back into society. He started his degree course again from the beginning along with fellow students considerably younger than himself, a situation which troubled him, feeling as he did that the life-threatening illness had matured him, given him wisdom and experience beyond his years that neither the younger students nor even those of the same age could understand.

He felt grown up. Very grown up. He wanted to take his life into his own hands. Together with two friends, he rented a little house in Coventry with a quiet back yard. He loved hanging up his hammock there in the sun and reading. He wallowed in the luxury of having his own room, decorating it lovingly with his books on philosophy and science fiction and of course his computer, rescued from its long sleep in Chris and Irene's attic.

The medics had already warned him that he would probably suffer concentration problems in the aftermath of chemotherapy and, indeed, he experienced the first months back at university as highly strenuous. However, his Director of Studies arranged flexible deadlines for him and everybody was as accommodating as possible, which went a long way to reducing the pressure.

Moving about within the disabled-friendly buildings caused him no difficulties and Alexander was delighted to find himself in immediate possession of an Orange Badge, allowing him to use disabled parking places. A huge relief, as Philipp had driven his car over for him and with crutches he couldn't walk far. A whole year passed at home before his disability pass was finally processed and it did not entitle him to use public parking facilities for the disabled.

By the time Ben flew over to visit his big brother for a week in November, a reunion that meant a lot to both of them, Alexander had recovered sufficiently to invite friends round for home-cooked lasagne, drive around the countryside for hours on end in his beloved car, sit up all night watching videos and could keep up fairly well with his studies. He was alive and kicking!

Once or twice a week he worked as a volunteer counsellor on a helpline for students who found themselves in problematic or conflicting situations or who were feeling suicidal. It was his way of passing on some of the support and care he himself had received.

Despite our protests, Alexander insisted on driving back to Germany for Christmas by car and via Hamburg. That had us worried. But it was his life, his decision.

How healthy he looked! Still underweight for his size, but well-padded compared to the months in hospital. His hair had regrown in thin, faint patches, but it was hair all the same.

The vexed question of aftercare hung over us. With Alexander's consent, I had booked an appointment for him in our hospital in Regensburg. Just the thought of it made him feel sick. The first two days of his visit he spent cowering in bed and eventually he admitted that so far he had not gone along for a single one of the closely monitored check-ups. He pressed his lips together firmly.

'Either I'll survive or it will come back, and then I'll die. Check-ups are humiliating.'

Just before Christmas, Ben discovered a lump on the back of his head. Our GP sent him off for a CAT scan. Ben was frightened. Having to wait in the same practice where his brother's bone cancer had first been imaged was harrowing. But he emerged from the examination room smiling with relief; the bump turned out to be a ganglion, somewhat unusual in that position, but nevertheless completely harmless.

Matters did not run so smoothly with Natty. At the start of the school year she had worked hard, come to us regularly for lunch, talked enthusiastically and generally made a stable impression. Then things started to crumble. She skipped classes, didn't turn up for exams, turned once again to drugs. Just one week before Christmas with the promise of roast turkey and bulging stockings, the situation reached crisis point and she went into the drug clinic for detoxification. She was given notice for her room. On Christmas Eve, she discharged herself on her own responsibility and disappeared.

We had won Alexander back again only to lose Natty. Christmas brought happiness, yes, but also pain and sadness. By the time Natty established contact with us again, Alexander had long since left.

We salvaged what we could. Natty stuck to her goal of sitting her *Abitur* or A-levels, but several marks were missing. A discussion with the headmaster confirmed she had only one chance left and that meant standing back for the rest of the year, using the time to catch up on the exams she had not written, and then start the thirteenth grade afresh in the autumn term.

So that was settled. Once she had found somewhere to live, Natty kept herself busy reading, occasionally helping me grow the vegetables and summer flowers, and even held down a holiday job.

At Easter, I flew to England. Alexander met me at the airport. He limped round the corner without crutches, smiled sheepishly and wrapped his arms round me. But he looked terrible. His thin hair hung limply and there was a sore on his lip. He seemed so gaunt that I bought him a large baguette on the spot.

Back in Coventry, he proudly showed me round his house, pretending to be surprised at the empty pantry in the kitchen. After a sumptuous feast in a restaurant, we drove over to the supermarket and bought enough provisions to feed a whole hospital.

Over the next three days, we inspected the computer science department at the university, the Warwick Arts Centre and landscaped gardens, went to the cinema and Alexander demolished enormous amounts of everything I cooked for us. Short distances on even ground he could manage without crutches and at a reasonable pace; but no more. His leg simply refused to bend more than 90 degrees.

No matter. He was evidently happy as he was. And especially so when we sought out our idyllic holiday cottage with its rose-clad stone walls, hobbled round the castle ruins and ordered his favourite meal in the cosy old pub he loved so dearly.

We saved the best for the end; a day outing to Lincoln! Alexander knew exactly where to find our secret parking place at the back of the Toy Museum and entrance to the castle. But the days when he could run with his brother and sister in ecstatic anticipation down 'Steep Hill' were gone forever; he pulled the crutches out of the car. I was terrified he would slip on the wet cobblestones.

But just as we set off, the rain stopped and the sun came out. Slowly and carefully, we picked our way down to our old friend the bookshop, 'Reader's Rest'.

He took his time, as always. From a safe distance, I watched him fingering the books on the floor-to-ceiling shelves, soaking up the faintly musty smell, delighting in coming across a hitherto undiscovered corner in the labyrinth of rooms, jokingly complaining to the shop assistant that somebody had moved the classic literature section so his search would take a little longer. I knew he was playing for time. When the Minster bells suddenly filled the city with their joyous peals, I thought my cup must overflow with happiness and cried amongst the tightly packed bookshelves.

The sun shone merrily as we drove back past fields full of sheep and their lambs, past suburban gardens, yellow with daffodils and narcissi, past gently undulating hills and fresh green grass. Alexander hummed as he drove, leaning his arm in a carefree fashion on the open window and laughing as the wind tousled his hair.

'This day,' he confessed with tears in his eyes, 'has been one of the best in my whole life.'

1 0

Relapse

At the end of his frequent e-mails regaling us with accounts of the pleasures of student life, such as a weekend trip to Dublin, a balmy day spent with friends on the shores of Rutland Water, a pub lunch in Kenilworth or a course assignment that fascinated him, Alexander routinely signed off with a quote from the philosopher Søren Kierkegaard: 'Life can only be understood backwards, but has to be lived forwards.'

With almost uncanny accuracy this sentiment summed up the long, wretched months in hospital, so much of which we did not begin to understand until afterwards. Feelings of guilt started to emerge.

I was especially troubled by the fact that I had quite underestimated the cost of living in Britain. I thought I was paying Alexander a handsome amount of maintenance money each term, and was astonished to hear that he could barely manage.

Not that he lived extravagantly. But his car not only counted as one of the highlights of his new life, it was also a basic necessity and he invested heavily in petrol. Visits to the theatre, cinema and music concerts kept up his spirits and compensated him for the long period of abstinence. He would have loved to have seen a play by a well-known theatre group, he told me afterwards when it was too late, but he hadn't been able to afford the entrance ticket. Such a small pleasure that was denied him. I reproached myself bitterly.

We had planned on treating Alexander (and ourselves) to a proper holiday in the summer because, apart from the sprint to Bulgaria, none of us had enjoyed a real break since his illness had begun and now at last we saw the chance to rectify the situation. Alexander was much looking forward to it. But at the same time, he dreamt of a summer job in America selling ice cream and we understood the hint that he was his own master again and could fend for himself.

Only it didn't work out like that. Shortly before his final exams started in May, Alexander rang home. There was something wrong with his leg; a lump had formed at the top of his thigh and every step made him wince with pain. He was going to see a consultant at The Royal Orthopaedic Hospital in Birmingham.

He sounded matter-of-fact, almost resigned. We were shocked. When he phoned again a few days later to give us the latest news, we had gone through the depths of despair. Now I could detect relief in his voice. The X-rays had revealed nothing unusual in his lungs. Rather, the root of the thigh problem had been identified as a purely mechanical one. The enormous pressure on the upper section of the prosthesis had caused it to loosen slightly. The resulting friction had further eroded the bone tissue, which in turn had put even more weight on the bolts until they had eventually snapped. In fact, the lump he could see on his thigh was the broken head of one of the bolts. It meant another operation and as soon as possible. Until then Alexander was warned not to use that leg at all.

'Mum, this is going to be a tricky job, so I want to come home. Would you mind making the arrangements, please? And by the way, it might mean an amputation.'

Amazing how sensible and reasonable he had become. No 'I can cope better on my own', just a modestly factual appraisal of the situation.

The co-ordination between the two hospitals was exemplary, with the X-rays from Birmingham arriving within days. Alexander's surgeon put our minds at rest – the damage could be repaired! Tell Alexander not to worry, but finish his exams at Warwick first and then come over to Germany, he said. His leg would last that long, no doubt about it.

So Alexander sat all his tests in business studies and computer science and completed his first year at university without further mishap. In June he drove back home on his own in the car, in his luggage a belated birthday present for me: a book as usual. He watched me expectantly as I unwrapped a copy of Joseph Heller's classic *Catch 22*.

'You know of course that the phrase "catch 22" originates from the book, but you really must read the novel if you want to find out exactly what it means.'

With the click-clack of his crutches on the floor, there was no mistaking his presence in the house. Wolfgang suggested he should get new walking aids as the old ones squeaked with over-use, but Alexander would hear nothing of the sort. His crutches had character, he said, and he refused to be parted from them.

He asked me to go with him to the appointment with the surgeon, 'in case I don't take it all in' as he put it. I knew what he meant. Simply the sight of the hospital complex induced a heaviness in mind and body. Once inside, the sight of white-gowned staff, endless corridors, the banging of the dinner trolleys and smell of disinfectant, the glimpses of old, ashen-looking men and women in their beds, brought back the old familiar feeling of deep fatigue. For the second time we sat down in the surgeon's office, discussed once again how to salvage his limb. It all seemed so grotesquely familiar.

Alexander had three choices: an amputation, a stiff leg without a knee joint or experimental surgery with a new endo-prosthetic replacement. The latter idea was geared to lending his leg more stability by transplanting a live donor bone, through which the surgeon would insert an extended prosthesis, like an arm in a sleeve. With any luck, the transplanted tissue would in time knit together with the ends of Alexander's own bone. If that succeeded, then it would be possible at a future date to replace his artificial knee joint with a live donor one, thus greatly improving his mobility.

And while they were at it, the surgeon added, they could stretch his leg, which had emerged from the previous operation 2 cm shorter, to make it the same size as the other one. But nobody was guaranteeing anything. The transplant might not take and, as each additional operation inevitably eroded more of the already hardly existent bone substance, a third attempt at limb salvation would probably be a failure. Alexander could expect to need crutches again for at least three months, perhaps longer.

He opted for the donor bone, cracked a joke about having all his iron reserves in his leg and asked politely if he might keep the old rod as a souvenir.

But first of all the surgeon had to wait for the prosthesis to be made to measure and for an accident victim with a valid donor card and healthy thigh to arrive in the morgue. The thought that somebody had to die before his own leg could be saved occupied Alexander's thoughts continually and, during the two-week wait, we spent hours discussing his feelings.

At last, everything was ready. None of us could imagine another prolonged spell in hospital. We hadn't yet recovered from the previous months. But we had no alternative.

Much to his embarrassment, Alexander found himself on the 'torture ward' again, in exactly the same room at the end of the corridor where he had screamed in agony after his first surgery. After this second lengthy operation, Alexander lay on his back in bed, a new 75 cm wound down his leg, two diagonal gashes across his hips where pieces of bone had been removed for transplant, more than 80 spidery-black stitches and an impressive array of ten drainage bottles and tubes.

This time round, however, he was in a better state, both physically and mentally. Nevertheless, having to lie helplessly again in bed, attached to the drip and morphine pump, surrounded by vivid memories, totally dependent on outside help, understandably taxed his patience. He tried heroically not to annoy the staff too much. In return, they pretended diplomatically to have forgotten the ugly scenes of a year earlier.

Time passed slowly in the sweltering room. The hot June sun blazed relentlessly through the window. All too quickly, we fell back into old habits. We sat with Alexander in shifts, tried to amuse and distract him. We made up stories, caught up with our news of the last months. Alexander dreamt of the future. In the *next* summer holidays he wanted to travel to South Africa or Portugal, and when he had gained his degree at Warwick, he would then study artificial intelligence at the Massachusetts Institute of Technology in America. We counted the days, hours, minutes and seconds until discharge.

'Natty has a split personality,' he mused one day, 'and I have a split body. One half belongs to someone else and the other half consists of metal.'

It was quite true. Not only did Alexander possess an iron will, he was a walking scrapyard. When a nurse handed him over the old endo-prosthesis, clinically clean and packed fetchingly in a transparent bag, we were all amazed. An impressive 33 cm long, it weighed a hefty 1250 g. No wonder Alexander had gained weight in record time. Only it wasn't due to the mountains of baked beans at all, but the titanium rod in his leg!

Two or three nurses from oncology popped over to visit Alexander, a gesture which he very much appreciated. Both of the ward doctors from the previous year had left the hospital in the meanwhile. We missed them dreadfully.

After 14 long days, Alexander could come home. And start all over again. Due to the lack of exercise, the muscles on his legs had wasted away visibly and he could hardly move, let alone drive the car. So we rented the time-tested CPM again, strapped the poor thin, stitched-together leg into it twice a day and watched it being gently exercised. Every day the drive to physiotherapy, where his favourite therapist worked with him again. Alexander had to learn how to walk all over again. Progress was slow and, although both Ben and Natty and other friends supported him to the best of their ability, he seemed increasingly dispirited and demoralized.

Two days after his discharge from hospital, visitors arrived. We had been planning the week for a very long time and couldn't bear to cancel or postpone it. But whilst the family enjoyed outings together, Alexander tried to catch up on his sleep. Going with us or even sitting with us at the table was nothing but wishful thinking. In a feeble attempt to bring him back just a little into the family fold, we fixed up a provisional bed for him outside next to the garden table.

Not that he complained. On the contrary, he bore the new drudgery with courage. But he was pale, quiet and subdued. As an incentive, we offered him a weekend break in the Czech Republic. Natty was working at her summer job and Ben had other plans, so we suggested just the three of us should go. Alexander was thrilled. He looked much brighter.

Český Krumlov is a sleepy little town coiled along the river and bursting with asymmetrical medieval houses, artists' galleries, student pubs, grand piazzas and cobblestoned lanes, all at the foot of the magnificent castle with its famous frescoes. After a three-hour drive with breaks for lunch and to rest, we reached the old part of the town and took up quarters in a cheerful family room in a guesthouse with disabled access and a view over the Moldau.

The journey had worn Alexander out. While he rested, Wolfgang and I set off on an exploratory walk and discovered a student pub quite close by, cosily decorated with candles and red checked tablecloths. In the evening, Alexander limped painfully back with us over the slippery cobblestones, glad that we had quickly found places to sit amongst the laughing students and home-baked pizza as well.

Soft white rolls, coffee and hot chocolate on the breakfast tray reminded us of a family trip to Prague many years before. Alexander made up his mind to see at least some of the tourist attractions despite the blisters that hurt his hands. Step by step, we walked slowly along with him, resting every five minutes and taking frequent breaks at the pavement cafes dotted all around us. Lunch at the riverside, poking around in the art galleries, people-watching in the elegant squares, soaking up the warm August sun, writing postcards to friends – those were blissful hours together.

Only one thing spoiled our pleasure. Alexander longed to see the inside of the castle with his own eyes, but the steep approach to the entrance gates defeated him. He gave up, stayed behind in the room on his own and awaited our description of the fortress. Periodically he mentioned that his right hip – not the freshly operated leg – was hurting. When Wolfgang and I returned after an evening stroll, we found our son fully dressed and asleep on the bed. He did not wake up until the following morning.

The ache refused to go away and Alexander was still swallowing painkillers well after the operation. After putting up with it for a while longer, he decided to pop over to the hospital for a check-up, a move which encouraged me to hope that he might just have a change of mind regarding the aftercare programme.

Nobody could find anything wrong. The pain was attributed to the strain of placing all his weight on one leg. Nothing to worry about. Alexander looked cheerful when he came back.

While he busied himself with planning his return to England and new digs in Coventry, Wolfgang, Ben and Natty went back to school. After almost a year's absence, Natty understandably felt apprehensive. She needed all the courage and initiative she could muster. On the first morning, Ben and I picked her up from her flat, pressed a sugar pig into her hands to bring her good luck, hugged her and escorted her to school.

Phone calls in the evening and visits at lunchtime persuaded me that everything was running fairly smoothly and, with each day that passed, we grew more confident in our daughter's ability to settle down and find her place in the school community.

Summer was coming to an end. For the second year running, we, but most especially Alexander, had spent a considerable part of it cooped up in stifling rooms in hospital, at home or in the physiotherapy studio. The longed-for recuperation had evaded us yet again.

On 17 September we celebrated Alexander's twenty-second birthday. Although not a lavish affair in a material sense, it lacked nothing in closeness and love as all five of us gathered round the birthday candles. Alexander had requested a scanner as a present, so the next day we drove to the shop and he hopped up and down the aisles on his crutches, frowning with concentration as he studied the various models before making his choice. We carried the unwieldy box back to the car for him.

19 September – Ben's eighteenth birthday! Mum and Dad were courteously but firmly requested to leave the house for 'health reasons' – Ben had invited at least 20 mates to a party – and stay overnight with friends. Alexander was not forcibly evacuated; on the contrary, Ben was proud to have his big brother with him.

When we arrived home the next day, diplomatically making sure we didn't appear until early afternoon, the house was spick and span. Just to make sure, Ben had called in the next-door neighbours to approve the post party clean-up, and both boys were flushed with excitement and lack of sleep.

Without crutches Alexander was helpless, but that did not deter him from driving the car back alone to England the next morning. We knew better by now than to argue. Laboriously, he and I carried his clothes, his latest literary acquisitions and boxes of computer accessories to the car, checked the oil, made sandwiches and pinned the map onto the dashboard.

He looked well. A little pale, perhaps, but well. I asked him how his hip felt and he shrugged his shoulders, saying nonchalantly that he still needed the painkillers. I begged him to go for another check-up as soon as he arrived back at university. I felt very uneasy that there had been no improvement. Tall and straight he stood there, smiling at me coyly. When I started crying, he put his arms around me.

'Course I will. But I'm fine, Mum, honestly. Don't worry about me.'

Then he clambered into the car, half dragging, half lifting his leg inside, stuck his hand through the open sunroof, called 'See you at Christmas' and drove off.

Whether he ever did consult a doctor remained unclear. In his e-mails he made no further mention of his hip. Instead, he wrote exuberant accounts of his second-year course which was meeting his wildest dreams and hopes, and repeatedly told us how happy and content he was.

He derived much pleasure from his new abode. Together with three friends, he had moved into a semi-detached house where he occupied a room on the ground floor. With tangible delight, he described in detail how his bed fitted so neatly into the corner of the room that he could see both his bookshelf and the birds outside in the garden. The only drawback was that he had to climb a set of steep stairs to reach the bathroom on the first floor. Otherwise he couldn't have been happier.

At last, at long last, we could entertain realistic hopes that our shattered lives would get back on track: all five of us were more or less well and living where we wanted to be. After all the dreadful stress and tension, we were gasping for a period of normality, just to get us through daily life. Both Natty and Ben found themselves at a critical phase of their school careers and had to sit innumerable exams, all of which counted towards the final *Abitur* mark.

The first half of October passed uneventfully. Natty was coping well, beginning to shake off her initial nervousness, showing renewed interest in school life and keeping in close contact with us. Ben had settled down to life in the 12th grade and was concentrating on his special subjects.

For me, the winter term began with six classes and I was busy reuniting existing groups after the summer break and encouraging new ones to bond.

One evening, shortly before the autumn break, the phone rang. It was a friend of Alexander's. With carefully selected words, she explained that Alexander had been admitted to the local hospital's casualty department where they discovered that his leg – the right one, not the operated one – was broken. A fatigue fracture or something. Apart from that, he was just fine. He sent his love and we were not to worry. She would contact us again as soon as she knew more.

We tried to think through the consequences of this new mishap. As Alexander could not yet place his full weight on the recently operated left leg, a fractured right one meant total incapacity. There would be no alternative to a wheelchair. We agreed that I should fly over to England in the half-term holiday and assess the situation on the spot. Wolfgang booked a return flight for me.

The next evening, Alexander rang in person. He didn't have much more to tell us except that he was lying in a room with 22 other patients in a hospital in Coventry which was about to be demolished, but that his friends were taking great care of him. He was really just fine and – his voice sounded insistent – there was absolutely no reason for me to come over whatsoever. He had everything under control.

I told him I was coming anyway, but that he would have to wait until the end of the week when my classes finished and I could get away for a few days.

This new development presented us with more trials and tribulations. And we felt uneasy. But we didn't panic, carried on with our daily routine much as before. I bought a few more boxer shorts for Alexander – to be on the safe side.

My conversation class on Wednesday evenings always terminated the week's teaching. That night, nearly all the students had turned up and the atmosphere in the classroom was one of expectant curiosity.

We warmed up with a partner-finding activity. Everybody received a photo of half of a house mounted on a card and the idea was to find the partner with the missing part. That had to be solved by asking pertinent questions in English, however, and not just waving around the picture!

That done, we checked the vocabulary used and moved on to the next step – designing a dream house in teamwork. Hot debates followed, then outlandish sketches, peals of laughter, new creative suggestions, giggles. The respective groups were so engrossed in comparing their finished products that they were genuinely surprised by the bell. Quite spontaneously the class started clapping. What a lovely evening.

I took the image of their happy faces and the sound of laughter home with me. About an hour later, while I was packing my suitcase for my flight the next morning, the phone call came. It was Alexander. He said I should sit down.

Slowly and carefully, he explained that he had been moved from Coventry to the Royal Orthopaedic Hospital in Birmingham. The doctors had put him through the MRI scan. The image had shown that it wasn't so much his leg that was fractured, but his right hip. And it wasn't a fatigue fracture either. No. A new tumour had formed there and had cracked the bone from the inside.

He paused for a few seconds. And that wasn't all. He had a number of metastases, some of them the size of mandarin oranges, in both lungs.

He spoke with no great emotion.

'It's the end. The doctors have already explained it to me. They cannot do any more for me. Mum, I'm dying.'

1 1

Winding Down

It was dark when I arrived. After a night of anguished weeping, a guarded farewell to Ben who was sitting an important exam that morning and whom we did not want to initiate until afterwards, a phone call to organize replacement teachers for my classes, and a dash to the GP, Wolfgang saw me onto the plane headed for England.

At Birmingham airport, three of Alexander's friends were waiting for me, a welcoming bouquet of flowers in their hands. They had come with Alexander's car and drove me to the hospital which lay slightly set back from the busy main road in a woodland clearing. 'Royal Orthopaedic Hospital' said the sign in large letters at the entrance. Next to it a smaller notice: 'Specialist Bone Cancer Unit'.

Together we walked up to the ward. My arrival was expected. A nurse greeted me at the entrance with a hug. She thought it would be best if we had a cup of tea together first. Then she would take me to see Alexander.

While she busied herself with the tea ritual – 'You will take sugar, won't you? It's so good for shock' – she introduced herself as Alexander's named nurse and checked to see what I already knew. So far, she told me, he was taking the news well. She talked repeatedly about 'quality of life' and stressed more than once that the hospital would be there to help Alexander and me now – and afterwards. She had already reserved a room for me in the adjacent Nurses' Home where I could stay for as long as I wished. I just had to pick up the key.

She suggested sitting down again together in the next couple of days. Then she would take the time to go through further information with me, such as patients' leaflets about osteosarcoma, the addresses and phone numbers of national cancer organizations, counselling services and self-help groups. The hospital's own Macmillan nurse and social worker would contact me the following day, she added.

She was friendly and the conversation constructive. The feeling of abject misery and panic lifted somewhat. By the time we had emptied the teapot, I felt strong enough to face the next step. Alexander occupied a place in the main bay, a light-filled and spacious open-plan ward with eight beds spread over two optically separated sections. The nurse promised to move Alexander's bed into a side-room so we could be alone.

Alexander had retreated behind his flowery curtains. It was no good. As soon as I set eyes on him, I burst into tears. Deftly, the nurse pushed the bed round the corner and I stumbled after her.

Take your shoes off, she suggested. Make yourself at home. Move the beds to suit yourselves. She stayed with us until she was sure that we wanted to be alone. Alexander's friends had trooped off to collect the keys for my room from the concierge, find a vase for the flowers and space in the fridge for the food they had thoughtfully bought me.

Normally Alexander loathed people weeping because of him. I apologized and still could not stem the torrent.

'Mum, cry all you want. It's okay, really it is. Just cry. And come here. I want to cuddle.'

While I sobbed brokenly, he stroked me calmly and composedly. His broad neck. Shoulders and arms strong and muscular. His skin warm. I thought of the day when it would be cold to the touch.

He talked. The doctors had broken the news to him the night before and made it abundantly clear that nothing, no chemotherapy, nothing at all, would be of any use. They could, however, do a lot to maintain his quality of life until the end. One suggestion was to replace the fractured hip with an artificial one. With a bit of luck, he might be able to sit, perhaps even walk with crutches. Sit in a wheelchair? By now even that seemed eminently desirable. Each new setback lowered his expectations.

For Alexander it had been of tantamount importance to know how much time he still had left. Obviously the consultants could only hazard a guess. It would not be the tumour in his hip that would ultimately lead to his death, they said, but the secondaries in his lungs. Twelve months at best. But nobody really knew.

Alexander appreciated the honest but empathetic and gentle way the doctors broke the news. He was equally grateful that they had then not left him alone with his death sentence but called in Alexander's named nurse who had stayed with him, talking to him, comforting him, cuddling him, and had done her utmost to relieve his emotional pain (morphine tablets were controlling the physical side), until well into the night.

Already, Alexander had made plans. He was undecided whether to agree to the hip replacement operation, but he knew for sure that he wanted to stay in England, attend university, live as normally as possible. For the end, he wanted to come home to die, his family around him.

He had a dreamy air about him. As though he were far away.

'I'll just wind my life down slowly. I don't mind. Dying's all right. And should it get really bad, well, I'll just take an overdose,' he added with a knowing, unperturbed smile.

He seemed so composed and at peace that I could say goodnight to him with a clear conscience. The girls showed me the way to my room and I fell asleep immediately.

In the morning, we talked things over again in the light of day. Alexander repeated his decision not to undergo any further chemotherapy under any circumstances, not even if a course of treatment could conceivably extend his life or offer him the outside chance of survival.

Yet he had changed. The jagged edges had been worn down. He was soft and relaxed as never before. His constant need to touch, be stroked and cuddled, surprised me. I reminded him of how unresponsive he had been as a baby and he laughed and said, well then, it was high time he caught up now.

'I want everything settled. Then I can die in peace,' and he apologized for a couple of occasions in the past when he had behaved badly. Could I forgive him? As an answer, I gave him a big hug.

He talked about love. Something unexpected had happened. Just the day before he had been admitted to hospital, Alexander had met a charming girl at a student party and, although he had always claimed obstinately that he would never fall in love again, he was clearly smitten.

The girl came to visit every day and Alexander made it quite clear that they wanted to be alone. His eyes shone when she walked into the room and after she had left, he loved talking about her and listing their many common interests.

'She is very special to me,' he confided. 'I never thought I'd feel this way about a girl again.'

How bittersweet that he could love again, but with so little time left to enjoy it.

Rarely had I seen him so happy. He lay on his back surrounded by friends from all over the world. They spoke Farsi and Urdu and Chinese and German and English, they hugged him and massaged him, snuggled up next to him in bed and spoilt him with home-made Tandoori meals.

'Mum, I'd like you to meet all my friends. They are so cool.' Then to the students: 'And this is my Mum. She's cool too!' I was very touched.

Even more moving was the young people's sensitivity. They offered to leave the room if I wanted to be alone with Alexander. I didn't. Their presence and that of other visitors, such as Chris and Irene, or the local volunteers who sacrificed some of their time each day to talk to the patients, was nothing but a blessing, both for me and for Alexander. The constant stream of visitors filled Alexander with pride.

'Did you see how many came today? At least ten. You know, I was always a little jealous of Ben. He seems to make friends so effortlessly, unlike me. Well, now look – I'm surrounded by friends, real ones! This is where I belong. They understand me. I've found my feet, at last. This is my home, this is where I want to live.' And he leaned back on the pillow with an expression of sheer rapture on his face.

Of course the young people knew the score. But here and there the news had not yet got through. Alexander thought long and hard about how best to break the news to each person, tried to guess how they would react and considered who from his circle of friends could, if necessary, assume a counselling function.

It was like reading his own obituary. Being able to tell his friends himself, in his own words and in his own way, gave him immense satisfaction. He watched them closely, committed their remarks to memory, worried about them and in so doing helped himself as well, because he called the shots, he held the reins, he kept control over his life.

As with the next decision. Should he opt for a hip replacement, yes or no? We discussed the matter at length. If he took no action, he would lie flat on his back in bed until he died. If he consented, the same fate might befall him. A course of radiation treatment afterwards would be needed to reduce the risk of rogue cancer cells in his hip spreading. But the consultants felt optimistic that, after surgery, Alexander would at least be able to sit if not walk. Altogether they expected him to stay for another eight or ten days in the clinic.

The university authorities were exemplary in their efforts for us, offering both of us disabled living accommodation on the campus as soon as Alexander could be discharged. Every day, the occupational therapist stopped by to chat to the patients and Alexander and together they worked out what aids he would require – a highchair, raised toilet seat, correct type of wheelchair. She even arranged a preliminary delivery date. It was wonderful to have so much hassle taken off our hands.

But in the end, it was the financial handouts that clinched the issue. Alexander could not believe his good fortune when the hospital social worker suddenly presented him with two or three cheques from various charities, providing him with enough funds to finance a last holiday. Alexander was quite overwhelmed at such unexpected generosity and hesitated to accept.

But the social worker persuaded him to keep it – 'Alexander, students are by definition impoverished!' – and also informed him that he would be eligible for a monthly allowance from the State until he died. Of course we parents had already promised to increase his maintenance payments, but this made Alexander feel unpleasantly in our debt. The living allowance was neutral and did not mean a loss of face.

So he agreed to the operation. While we waited for the prosthesis to be made, Alexander dreamt of his imminent discharge, continuing his degree course, going to the theatre and cinema, being at the heart of his circle of friends and spending weekend breaks in those European cities he had not yet visited. Vienna was top of the list. In the summer holidays ('I think I'll still be around by then, don't you?') he fantasized about hiring a car and touring South Africa.

You had to see him for yourself to understand his strange happiness, newly discovered gregariousness and need for friendship in this final phase. Wolfgang needed to judge the situation for himself. In the half-term break, he flew over for a few days.

He saw how Alexander's friends thought nothing of driving for an hour from Coventry to Birmingham in the afternoons and evenings, bringing with them bunches of balloons, colourful posters which they stuck up all over the walls, flowers and books and cuddly toys, a Jack o' Lantern for Halloween and their course assignments to discuss at considerable length with Alexander. There was not a shadow of doubt in his mind either that we should respect Alexander's wish to remain in England for as long as possible.

After the first appalling shock, it was slowly dawning on us that our son still had some living to do before he died. A few more days, and it seemed to us that a year was a long time yet. Anything could happen. After all, we encouraged each other, nobody knew the timetable for sure. Yes, it could be shorter. But it could also be longer. The more we thought about it, the more convinced we became that it would be longer. As far as the chemotherapy was concerned, Alexander did not change his mind. But we began to concentrate more on life, less on death.

The new hip had arrived. Alexander disappeared into the operating theatre. He showed no signs of distress, nor did he complain about the preliminary needle jabbing.

When I saw him again, it was in a curtained recess alongside other freshly operated patients in a ward called 'High Dependency'. Pale and in severe discomfort, attached to lines, drips, a morphine pump and various monitors, he lay there, his right leg resting in a wedge with a cushion to prevent it slipping. The sight did nothing for my morale. The only comfort was the sure knowledge that he was suffering this for the very last time.

The nurse on duty warned Alexander to make sure his leg did not tip to the side (which it did without fail if left to its own devices) as that would jeopardize his chances of walking again. This was nothing new to

us. Nevertheless, Alexander took the advice very seriously indeed. In a
jiffy, everything had reverted to the old routine. Alexander's leg kept
slipping. I tried to remove the cushion first – Alexander groaned and
whimpered with pain – and then to carefully shore up his poor thin leg
with it. It worked for a few minutes. Then the leg flopped over again and
we had to go through the same procedure again.

On the following day, Alexander had recovered sufficiently to be
moved back to the ward. But not to the quiet side room; to the bay.

Every single visitor and member of staff (and there were hundreds of
them, it seemed) had to walk through this area in order to reach the
nurses' station, doctors' room, dispensary, the women patients' section,
the toilets, bathrooms, linen store and medical equipment.

The decibel count from the catering staff alone could hardly have
been less than that of an international airport. Gaily, they trundled food
trolleys over the parquet floor several times a day. From one end of the
corridor to the other, people shouted to each other. Nurses trotted backwards and forwards endlessly, exchanging pleasantries with patients and
their relatives. Two communal television sets roared all day and well into
the night with football matches, car racing and *Emergency Room*. Some
patients preferred watching their own individual sets next to their beds.
Without headphones. Patients who were mobile could escape the noise
pollution when it became too much. Alexander could not.

On the other hand, the architecture encouraged an easy-going,
intimate atmosphere that stimulated social contacts which in turn offered
the base for friendship and mutual support and broke down isolation at
source. The two sitting rooms in the entrance area were cosily furnished
with armchairs, a television, videos and books, magazines and patients'
leaflets. Even though they complained that they were understaffed,
everybody working on the ward found time to sit down and chat freely to
the patients and their families.

Within an hour of arriving in the bay, Alexander was reduced to tears
of utter despair and begged to be moved to a quieter room. I asked the
nurse on duty. Sorry, not possible. Freshly operated patients, so the
hospital rules, must remain within eyeshot of the nurses' station so that
they can react quickly in an emergency. But she was willing to compromise. During her shift, she would allow Alexander to be moved to a side

room, providing I promised faithfully to stay with him at all times and
ring for assistance at the slightest sign of trouble.

Adjusting again to another hospital with its different regulations,
routines and ideology, most of which were unfamiliar to us, was not
always easy and occasionally led to misunderstandings.

It started, as so often, with the vocabulary. Whatever do you call the
thing hanging over the bed that you use to pull yourself up with? 'That?
Oh, it's a monkey pole!' the nurse said and looked surprised. We were
British, weren't we? So why didn't we know?

The furnishings in the rooms were simple: a small washbasin, a
bedside cupboard, a manually operated bed (which meant that Alexander
had to call for help whenever he needed to change position) with an
emergency button. Piped oxygen was an unheard-of luxury and cleanli-
ness did not take top priority.

Patients wanting to make a phone call had to ask for a pay phone on
wheels to be rolled to their bedside and incoming calls could only be
taken at the nurses' station and at their discretion. As Alexander could not
get up and walk there, the only solution was to push him along the
corridor and through the bay in his bed to the telephone. Wolfgang sent
us a mobile phone.

As all the patients on the ward, invariably young adults, suffered from
bone cancer, the discussions revolved round amputations, prosthetic
replacements and treatment protocols. Nearly every day, we witnessed
the new arrivals, tense and pale, but still with hope in their eyes. For the
first few days, we saw two feet on the floor next to the bed under the
closed, flowery curtains. Later only one.

Not realizing that he had been admitted to an oncological ward, an
older man asked Alexander one day whether he had broken his leg. The
reply shocked him into silence. Slowly he turned round and took in the
other young men and women. He looked at Alexander questioningly.
Alexander nodded. The man covered his face with his hands.

'Being on this ward makes you feel very humble,' he said, greatly
moved.

Patients, relatives, nurses and doctors all lived in close proximity. At
night, after we had 'put our relatives to bed', we walked back to the
Nurses' Home and gathered in the sitting room or kitchen or TV room.

We were always tired beyond belief. We sat together, swapping notes, crying, comforting each other, listening to accounts of the daily arguments (and reconciliations) that raged between despairing patients and helpless relatives, blowing up balloons for those with birthdays, sometimes drinking a glass of wine and laughing at silly little jokes to relieve the tension. I would have benefited even more if they hadn't all chain-smoked.

Occasionally the mood took a philosophical turn. One older woman with a terminally ill husband once summed up our feelings so: 'You cope with it every day and you get through it. But it takes over your life. There is nothing else. When you first get the diagnosis, you believe in a mix-up. Then you put your faith in the treatment. After that you pray for a miracle.'

Every morning, I walked the few yards between our respective buildings over to Alexander. The composure of the early days was starting to show faultlines and tempers flared easily. Overnight his whole frustration and hopelessness had built up and I took the brunt of it.

'Scientists can do all these wonderful things like growing new organs and limbs, but they can't help me.' Or: 'Mum, why did the cancer have to come back? Everything was going so well.'

I needed a change of scenery. Alexander's friends offered to drive me to the university to listen to a lecture and I accepted. I told Alexander that, just this once, I would be away for the afternoon. A shadow fell over his face and he snorted angrily.

'Oh, so you are just walking out and leaving me, are you?'

'Serves you right. You deserve to be left,' I snapped back, and didn't even regret it until I saw his face contort with misery.

He had every reason to be fractious. Despite repeated assurances that the operation had gone without a hitch, Alexander was making precious little progress. With a terrific effort and two people to support him, he could stand up – just – but he winced with pain. His right hip still hurt badly and his daily morphine ration of 350 mg surpassed that of the amputees. Staff began to hint that Alexander must be simulating, and that my maternal presence was encouraging this behaviour. Alexander moaned and groaned. I didn't know who to believe. Sometimes I felt furious towards this son who refused to get well again.

His appetite was poor. Swallowing became difficult and he could only eat soft foods. Breathing caused him no particular problems, but one morning he woke up to find that his voice had turned strangely squeaky.

By now it was November. Every day in hospital meant more precious living time lost.

But it still caught me unawares. I had come to keep Alexander company as usual. Squirming and fretting in his bed, he was complaining crossly that I couldn't even manage the simplest thing in the world – to straighten the pillow under his leg – when suddenly all the pain and fear and hopelessness erupted.

'If you really loved me, you wouldn't just sit there and let this happen to me,' he shouted hysterically. 'Go and get a gun and shoot me – that would be kinder than this. Go on! Kill me! I can't stand any more! Get out of here!' and he dissolved into a crumpled heap of hot tears.

I didn't know what to say. I wished I had a gun. He was quite right. This was nothing but torture. I stumbled out of the room straight into the arms of a passing nurse. She looked at me, asked whether I felt all right, and I muttered something about pistols and there being no point any more and then I couldn't see anything for tears. She took me firmly by the arm and propelled me along to the nurses' sitting room, pushed me down onto a sofa, put the kettle on and summoned the houseman.

But he didn't have any pistols for me either. 'There, there,' he said comfortingly and we drank tea. With sugar. Good for the shock. For Alexander, the nurse mobilized the Macmillan nurse and the social worker and his named nurse and anybody else who was available. Because they had all had contact with Alexander beforehand and built up a relationship to him, he was not ashamed to accept their help in the present crisis. Between the two of us, Alexander and I must have blocked the entire ward's resources for the rest of the day.

They did a marvellous job. It was a crisis long overdue, they soothed me. They had been expecting it. Now that it had happened, they said, the anger and fear exploded, things would be easier. And certainly, when I saw my son again the next day, Alexander struck me as being calmer. But also weaker and resigned.

Somehow we all moved on. Two days later, I glanced at his leg. The bandages were off, the wound clean and healing well. I was just admiring the stitches, when the flesh on his thigh suddenly bulged like a balloon when you blow it up. I couldn't believe my eyes. Alexander felt something too and turned to look. I rushed off to find a nurse, Alexander's own named nurse, as luck would have it. She ran back with me just in time to see for herself how the skin stretched and expanded.

'What is it?' Alexander wanted to know, but then answered his own question. 'It's a tumour, isn't it?'

The nurse admitted it was possible. But it could also be a blood clot, a haematoma. An ultrasound examination would bring clarity.

Two porters and another nurse accompanied Alexander, his bed and me down to the X-ray department. Alexander was terrified lest anyone should be rough with his leg. He was in agony and started to scream, the same anguished sound that he used to make when the primary tumour was eating away his left leg. But the staff were without exception very careful and gentle.

I sat outside with the nurse. The waiting was unbearable. If this was really another tumour, then I knew Alexander would not have long to live. I wept. The nurse held my hand. She told me that she had lost her baby son when he was a few months old and so she could well imagine how I must be feeling. I was glad to have her with me.

The ultrasound image proved inconclusive, but the doctors still suspected a haematoma. They wanted to operate again the very next morning. It would set Alexander back by a week, they thought. These things do happen sometimes.

So Alexander disappeared yet again into the theatre for nearly two hours, lost a lot of blood, spent the night in High Dependency, followed by a round in the bay and ended up back in the side room.

He endured everything with admirable stoicism and courage. And to start with, things did seem rosier. He could get to his feet and hold the pulpit frame – 'Goodness, Alex, we didn't realize you are so tall!' – and, after a couple more days, took his first wobbly steps on crutches. Staff and fellow patients clapped enthusiastically, shouted 'Good on you, son!' and Alexander grinned sheepishly. A message that his girlfriend was waiting for him in his room lent him wings – he almost danced back down the corridor.

But it didn't last. A week after the second operation, his thigh ballooned out again. This time nobody seemed keen to comment. We were told to wait and be patient.

The clock ticked away. Alexander's Director of Studies, who came every week to visit her student, kindly lent him her notebook so he could carry on writing his assignments for university. He had wanted that most of all. And he wanted them to be assessed. Brow furrowed in concentration, he typed away at an essay, researched in books, chewed his pencil thoughtfully or stared at the ceiling. I sat next to him and read. In the room it was quiet and peaceful. We lost all track of time and jumped with surprise when the evening meal arrived.

Sometimes we watched television. Every day, Alexander wrote in his journal. I treated him to his favourite magazines, an Advent calendar. More boxer shorts. A story, if I could think of one. It was all so inadequate. Yet as long as his friends visited him regularly – they did – and his mobile phone kept ringing – it rang – he felt well and happy, still belonged, had a quality of life.

Now it was December. The first students left for home. The dinner ladies sang 'Jingle Bells' in the canteen and the patients were looking forward to an early discharge. Nobody had been there as long as we had.

We had given up all hope of Alexander returning to university. Instead, we pinned all our hopes on flying home for Christmas, curing the haematoma, and then trying a new start back at university in January. The consultants confirmed that Alexander would soon be able to sit and cope with a flight. I booked tickets for both of us.

Only he didn't. He grew weaker and withdrawn. And the pain in his leg worsened with each passing day. Even though his daily dose of morphine tablets had been increased, he still suffered constant breakthrough pain and had to ask for additional morphine in liquid form. 'Could I have some Oromorph, please?' He was always polite. Using a very simple meditation technique taught to him by a fellow student, he tried to control the pain. Sometimes it worked. Sometimes it didn't. Then the trolleys thundered past, people laughed and joked and Alexander lay on his back behind his curtain and screamed with pain. I could not bear it any longer. I found the senior nurse and requested a doctor. Nobody ever came. I felt dreadfully alone and abandoned.

Problems of a different nature plagued another young man on the ward whom I often talked to. His heavily pregnant wife had visited him twice and stayed in the Nurses' Home, and now the bill – really quite reasonable – had arrived. He stared unbelievingly at the letter and confessed quietly to me that he couldn't pay it; his illness had eaten up their savings and he was too embarrassed to ask for charity. I was shocked.

I walked back down the corridor in a daze to Alexander and, while I told him the story, he pulled something out of his drawer and started writing. It was a cheque.

'Give this to him and ask him to accept it from me. Try and explain that I would love nothing better than to do some good in this world before I have to leave it.'

I was so proud of him! And despite his reservations, the man accepted the present. The next day he hobbled along on his crutches to visit Alexander. The two of them cried and hugged. Alexander was radiant with happiness.

But he couldn't fly. He couldn't even sit. Gradually the hospital emptied, the social worker was away on leave, the doctors avoided us and I grew desperate. How was I supposed to get Alexander home? It was a nightmare.

'Mum, I'll never get out. I'll die here,' he said, small and frightened and helpless.

Eventually, he solved the problem himself when he checked to see whether his membership with a German automobile association covered a repatriation by air ambulance. It did. In the coming days he would be flown back to Germany in a Lear jet. I couldn't go with him; I had to leave on the pre-booked charter flight.

The university term ground to a halt. Alexander's friends and Director of Studies came one last time to say goodbye. They brought him Christmas presents wrapped in love, cuddles and tears. His girlfriend came on her own later and stayed with him until late at night.

'Don't leave me here alone, Mum, please. What will I do if the plane doesn't come?'

But I had no choice. I hated having to stroke his tear-stained face, go without him. Two months after my arrival, I walked back out of the hospital gates and flew home alone. One of Alexander's friends promised me faithfully not to leave his side until the plane came. But when would that be?

The Last Weeks

Winter came early that year. Already the ground was frozen and at night there was severe frost. The outlook for a white Christmas seemed good.

At home, Ben had as usual displayed the first Christmas cards on the dresser and bookshelves. Despite, or perhaps because of, the extenuating circumstances, neither he nor Natty could help but be caught up in the seasonal cheer. Only another ten days until the school holidays and our last Christmas together.

The morning after I came back, I dashed into town, intending to buy a few presents for the children's stockings. Without the familiar hospital routine I felt strangely disorientated, and the shopping expedition only made matters worse. What can you give a dying son who can hardly eat or drink, cannot sit and cannot walk? And what do you give to the distraught siblings?

Before I had had time to take stock of what food was in the house, unpack, or sit down for a proper chat to Wolfgang, Ben and Natty, the automobile association rang to say that they would be fetching Alexander the next day from Birmingham, flying him back to Germany and taking him directly to our hospital in Regensburg. Some good news for a change! Alexander's thin voice cracked with relief when I called him to pass on the message.

But 24 hours later it was my turn to tremble at the end of the phone when Alexander rang me to announce his arrival at home in a few minutes, and not, as we had expected, at the hospital. An ambulance pulled up in front of the house, the paramedics staggered inside with Alexander on a stretcher and somehow even managed to carry him upstairs and deposit him on his bed in his room. Then they disappeared again.

Wonderful though it was to have him back with us, the unexpected-ness of his presence at home posed not a few problems. True, Alexander possessed enough morphine tablets to see him through the week at the current dosage, but his thigh was grotesquely swollen, causing his leg to twist and his foot to tip over limply. That worried him. He repeatedly poked around with his crutch in an attempt to position the little cushion from the living room sofa with the green silk cover under his leg. We had no equipment at all at home to cope with an invalid. Nor did I know what would happen next or where I might turn for help.

Alexander didn't really care. He was ecstatically happy to have side-stepped hospital and to find himself back at home, enjoying at long last the peace and privacy of his own room. We learnt that the air-ambu-lance team had indeed delivered him to the casualty department in hospital, where a doctor who did not know him had asked whether he wished to be discharged. Of course he did. So they had simply sent him on – just like that. Alexander pleaded with us please, please, not to send him back.

Just one night on his bed at home caused him unbearable pain. I had to cope with him on my own in the morning as the rest of the family was away at school. We agreed that I might call in the GP to assess the situa-tion.

He did not like the look of the puffed-up leg any more than I did, but he sympathized with Alexander's fear of ending up in hospital yet again, so he suggested taking him to a specialist surgery where a colleague could examine the haematoma and, if at all possible, puncture it there and then. Alexander agreed to the compromise; the pain was wearing him down.

We called an ambulance and, with the greatest care, the men carried Alexander down the stairs. But he still screamed with pain. Very solici-tously and slowly, doing their utmost to avoid bumps and jolts on the road, they drove him and me to the surgery where our GP was already waiting for us. His colleague gently touched the distorted thigh, thick and solid compared to the rest of the wasted body. Carefully, they pushed him over to the X-ray room.

Our GP sat down next to me in the waiting room. It was a marvellous feeling, knowing I wasn't alone any more. Alexander's ear-piercing screams went right through me. I thought I wouldn't be able to bear it any longer.

Then it was all over. They brought him back, white as chalk and exhausted from pain and crying. The doctor sat down on a chair and looked straight at Alexander while explaining gently that he could do nothing to help him and he would advise him to go to hospital.

No, no. Not hospital. Anything but hospital. Alexander looked so terrified that the doctor relented.

'We'll do a blood test, then. If the results are reasonable, you can go home. But if they are dodgy, I shall have to insist on sending you to hospital.' Alexander had no choice. He whimpered as the needle pricked his arm.

By now, it was late. The surgery had long since closed its doors and was, apart from the receptionist, deserted. She rang for a taxi to take the blood sample to the laboratory. Our GP waited with us the whole time. It seemed an eternity until the phone rang. The doctor shook his head. He was terribly sorry, he said, but the results were so poor that on medical grounds he simply could not allow him to go home. It was too dangerous. He would have to insist on sending him to hospital.

Alexander sobbed brokenly and turned to me with a pleading look that said, do something, help me. But I didn't. I couldn't. I was frightened and dog-tired and completely out of my depth. At home I had no equipment, no qualified help. Secretly, I was relieved to hear he was going back to hospital.

As on the previous day, he ended up in casualty. People in white coats rushed around hectically, demanding more X-rays and muttering darkly about an emergency operation. Alexander had regained his composure. He talked to me, but at a distance, as though I had nothing to do with him. It was ten in the evening and I had to leave him there on his own.

In the morning, I left the house after the others had gone to school, crossed the little footbridge over the motorway and looked for my son. Finally I discovered him, not in oncology, but on a newly renovated surgical ward. Nobody had operated, nor did Alexander know why, nor did anyone offer to give us any information.

At least the surroundings were pleasant. Quiet, airy and clean, the two-bed room boasted its own bathroom, white televisions on wall brackets, and personal telephones complete with internet connection by the bedside. It seemed the lap of luxury after the outdated furnishings in the Royal Orthopaedic Hospital in Birmingham. Alexander clutched the remote control for his bed just in case, as though afraid it might turn out to be nothing more than a figment of his imagination.

Waiting until Christmas to give him the only present we could think of that promised to give him some pleasure seemed perverse, so we brought him his parcel that same day. When Alexander had peeled a notebook out of the layers of wrapping paper, he let out a yelp of delight, just as he did all those years before at Christmas with his very first computer. Now he could phone or e-mail his friends at the flick of a switch or amuse himself playing games.

Nurses came and went. They were polite and did their duty, but nobody stopped to talk to Alexander about how he was feeling and they avoided Wolfgang and me completely. Three days passed before a nurse delivered a message to us, saying that the surgeon wished to speak to us.

The office had a sober feel to it, with its large desk, smoked-glass coffee table, black leather sofa and matching armchairs. We sat down opposite each other. He apologized for the long silence, explaining that he had needed the time himself to think things over. He coughed, embarrassed.

What we had believed to be a particularly stubborn haematoma was, he told us, only partly a blood clot. Most of the swelling consisted of a new tumour, which had developed out of cancer cells left over from the growth removed from his hip, and which was now wrapping itself around the new prosthesis in rings like an onion. Nothing could arrest its growth.

The surgeon had already played through all eventualities; amputating the leg would not guarantee catching all the malignant cells, and anyway, what would be the point of subjecting Alexander to such suffering when the deadly metastases lingered in his lungs? These had now reached such a size that they were pressing on Alexander's oesophagus. It wouldn't be long now before he would start fighting for breath.

He advised against chemotherapy, stressing that it would achieve nothing, nothing at all. Although he considered it unlikely that a course of palliative or symptom-reducing radiotherapy would have any effect, he thought we might like to give it a try. He had asked his colleagues from oncology and radiotherapy to join him and discuss the matter with Alexander.

He couldn't say how much time our son had left. Older patients died quickly because their hearts could not take the strain, but the youngsters, well, their hearts were strong. Yes, he had already spoken to Alexander in person. We could leave him on the surgical ward until the end, he offered. He was really so terribly sorry. Then the interview was over.

Why? Why couldn't Alexander be granted even those last few months of life? I couldn't feel the ground under my feet any more. As in a trance, we withdrew to the sitting room on the ward, collapsed onto the stylish blue sofa and wept. Wolfgang recovered first and went off to see how his son was feeling. I followed him later.

Alexander was concerned. Not for himself, but for us. Instinctively he'd known all along that it was another tumour and he was relieved to find his gut feeling confirmed, himself rehabilitated. If anything frayed his nerves, made him cry with frustration, then it was the feeling that nobody ever took what he said seriously. Now everything was clear. He would just wait for the consultants' visit, then come home, as promised.

But the medics did not appear. Instead, Alexander was transferred to another room while workmen installed mini-bars and screwed wood panelling to the walls in his previous one. Alexander found himself sharing with a grossly overweight man and his garrulous wife. Through the window we had a view of men working on the building site of the new hospital wing. Cranes swung past, bulldozers thundered up and down, pneumatic drills screeched non-stop and at regular intervals we heard a dull thud as the next delivery of bricks hit the concrete floor.

Neither the room-mate nor his wife took any notice of us. In a loud, harsh voice, she complained incessantly, moaning bitterly about the deafening noise, incompetent nurses, doctors who were useless and cheeky cleaners and, when she realized that her husband's phone was out of order, reaching a state little short of hysteria.

Alexander needed to pee. He asked politely and more than once if she wouldn't mind leaving the room shortly before she showed any reaction. Grumpily, she stomped out, demonstratively banging the door shut behind her. Alexander missed his bed curtains dreadfully. Using a bedpan in full view of other patients was distasteful to him in the extreme and he swore not to have any more bowel movements until he was in the privacy of his own home.

People kept bursting into the room unannounced. Or, even worse, they just turned the handle on the door, but never actually opened it, and disappeared without even having set foot inside. It drove Alexander mad. He kept a record over a 24-hour period of the number of intrusions and arrived at no less than 180 entrances or handle turnings!

As soon as his cantankerous wife had finally departed, the room-mate fell asleep sitting up in his bed. His vast stomach heaved rhythmically as he snored with a velocity that had the floor vibrating and the medicine bottles rattling. We watched as he sucked in the air, then held his breath for so long that we thought he must surely be dead. When, to our surprise, he did suddenly breathe out, the imprisoned air exploded with such concentrated force that it dislodged his false teeth, banning them to the edge of his fleshy lips where they quivered in expectation of being catapulted against the wall opposite. But at the last moment, he sucked them back in to his mouth again and the whole procedure started from the beginning.

Alexander rang for a nurse and asked to be given ear plugs. He did not complain. Just lay quietly dying in his bed. If he had said but one word, just one word, I would have called for an ambulance there and then and taken him home, away from this hell. But he didn't, and so we stayed.

We stayed until Alexander was moved back into the quiet room. Stayed until eventually the three consultants turned up at his bedside. Alexander listened to them attentively.

The oncologist said there was still hope. He had pulled a couple of patients through, he told us, and for that reason he was in favour of a small operation to re-implant a Hickmann catheter, followed by two or three rounds of high dose chemotherapy. Oh yes, and they would need to fatten him up a little, so time to switch to artificial nutrition.

The radiologist said he was hopeful that a course of radiotherapy could reduce the swelling of the tumour, a purely palliative measure, of course. Alexander wanted to know if it would hurt and was told, no.

The surgeon didn't say anything and looked at his shoes.

Alexander thanked them all and told them he did not want any more chemotherapy, did not want any life-extending treatment at all, but would be willing to give the radiotherapy a try. The oncologist thought Alexander should think everything over carefully. Maybe he didn't really understand what he was saying?

That made Alexander even more obstinate. For the first time, somebody was dangling a straw in front of our eyes and yet Alexander categorically refused to take hold of it. I wanted to clutch that last straw. For the next hour or so I discussed, pleaded and cajoled with him. All to no avail. He lay on his back, tears running down his cheeks.

'Mum, I'm not refusing to annoy. Please understand that I simply cannot take any more. And anyway, it would be pointless. You heard yourself what all the others said, what they said in Birmingham.'

He was, of course, quite right. I felt ashamed. There was nothing more to be said. All we wanted now was to get Alexander home, away from the needles, the opening doors, snoring room-mates, the smell of disinfectant.

In the afternoon, Wolfgang went shopping for a Christmas tree and a turkey. And he ordered a hospital bed with a remote control, a special mattress to combat bed sores, bought a little bedside table and unpacked the urine bottles and bedpans left over from the year before. Once the suppliers had delivered the bed on Christmas Eve and set it up in the living room – Alexander longed for his own bedroom upstairs, but it was too small to accommodate all the apparatus we knew would soon be necessary – we were prepared.

On 24 December, the hospital sent him home, just as it had two years previously. He arrived by ambulance with enough morphine tablets for the rest of the week and a discharge letter for our GP who was already on his two-week holiday. No sign of the social services. We had made it clear

on several occasions that, apart from coming in as an outpatient for radiotherapy sessions, Alexander would never again stay in hospital.

There was so little time. Alexander wanted the bed flat against the
wall, not sticking out into the room. Like that he felt safer, less conspicu-
ous. The frosted glass panel in the living room door troubled him as well.
Everyone can see me, he complained. There's no privacy. So I covered it
up with an old blue curtain and we didn't use that door at all, but entered
the living room via the kitchen and open doorway. No handles that had
to be turned. Alexander was content.

From his bed, he could look out of the big window on to the
snow-covered garden. We declared the living room Alexander's private
quarters; he was at liberty to throw us out as he wished. Within easy reach
on his bedside table stood the phone, from which he could alert us if he
needed help.

Natty and Ben decorated the lush and sweet-smelling Nordmann fir
while Alexander watched. Pretty, he said, appreciatively. Upstairs in my
bedroom, I hurriedly wrapped up the last small presents that I had
tracked down for the stockings. Christmas dinner was saved as well: for
the first time ever, we had to do without a home-made pudding, but at
least we could get by with the bought one I had carried back with me
from England.

We spent the evening as we always did, the parents in the kitchen
shelling chestnuts to stuff the turkey and the children trying to guess
what could be in their presents which were lying under the tree. They
carried Alex's pile over to his bed so he could touch and rattle and smell
and guess too. Natty decided to stay the night with us. I read them a
Christmas story and we watched a little television. We knew we were
doing these things together for the last time.

Late at night, I slid the not exactly numerous presents into the stockings, sad that they fitted easily into the red patchwork legs which did not
threaten to burst at the seams as usual. In the early hours of the morning,
while the family still slept, I crept down to the first floor with the stockings under my arm and distributed two outside Natty's and Ben's
bedroom doors. The third was for Alexander. He was breathing regularly
and, although fast asleep, gripping the remote control firmly in his hand.
Very quietly, I propped the thin stocking next to his fat leg.

On Christmas Day in the morning, we assembled in the living room round the tree to open stockings and presents, Ben and Natty happy and excited, the turkey roasting in the oven and the scent of candles filling the room.

But Alexander was in pain. His daily dose of 375 mg was suddenly unable to control the spasms of pain that constantly rocked through his body, leaving him gasping for breath and choking with tears. We gave him an extra tablet, but as they work on a slow release of 12 hours, we could expect no immediate relief. He tried opening his presents, but his shrieks were of pain, not delight, and the parcels fell to the floor.

Wolfgang rang the surgical ward in hospital and asked for help. Bring him back to us was the unequivocal reply. But we couldn't, not even temporarily. By now the pain was so severe that Alexander could not bear the slightest movement or touch. We took it in turns to sit next to him, holding his hand, mopping his brow, listening helplessly to his screams. He couldn't eat one spoonful of his Christmas dinner.

We rang the ward a second time. Ring emergency services, they suggested. So we dialled 999, described the situation and explained that we needed morphine – urgently. Shortly afterwards, a doctor arrived with a black case and no morphine. He did not know what to do, so he left again without doing anything.

Wolfgang rang the ward and for the third time informed them of our desperate position. Only then did we hear about the hospital's own pain control department and its emergency service.

At three o'clock in the afternoon – several hours after our first appeal for help – Dr N rang at the door, armed with plenty of morphine. He had been on call all day, but nobody had alighted him to our plight. It took half an hour to raise Alexander's morphine level from 375 to 1200 mg, at which point the pain dissipated as quickly as it had come. 'Can I open my presents now,' a tear-stained but recovered Alexander asked, 'and have some Christmas dinner?'

There wasn't much time left for us to savour that last Christmas day, but we etched on our memory those dark winter hours when Alexander's eyes sparkled in the candlelight, the way he fingered his new books lovingly or laughed with his brother at his new computer game and even ate a few spoonfuls of turkey and roast potato and Christmas pudding.

On New Year's Eve, Alexander had visitors. Philipp came to stay for three days, to say goodbye. Patiently, he sat next to his friend's bed, talking and chatting to the increasingly silent, ashen-faced shape lying there. In the evening, we pushed Alexander's bed over to the window so he could enjoy an uninterrupted view of the fireworks at midnight. We drank to his health and wished each other a happy New Year and knew perfectly well that it wouldn't be.

I wondered which day he would die on.

'Mum,' he asked one day, 'I shall never go back to England, shall I?'

His words cut through me like a knife. I looked at him.

'No. You will never see England again.'

The light drained out of his soft brown eyes and he nodded.

It was blissfully quiet at home. Outside the blanket of snow muffled the sound of traffic and inside we moved unhurriedly and with lowered voices. The weaker Alexander grew, the greater our need for peace and quiet. Simple meditation had soothed him before, now he asked for more personal tuition.

So the New Year started with a new routine. Every day, the meditation teacher came and sat with Alexander, guiding him through the steps and, when he had grasped the principle, meditating together with him. After each session, Alexander looked serene, relaxed and deeply content.

Less to his liking was the rearrangement of furniture that had become necessary. Having the bed next to the wall proved impractical, as I could only reach him from one side. Although Alexander continued to wash himself and we had long since given up trying to heave him to his feet for a walk (the pain was too intense), we had to make the bed more accessible. To compensate for this infringement on his liberty, we moved the sofa over to one side and the chairs to the other so he would not feel so exposed.

He was reluctant to admit it, but the new plan did mean we could all sit down comfortably with him. From his bed, he could admire the bouquets of spring flowers and potted plant arrangements that were delivered to the door nearly every day, follow the sun pace through the wintry sky, see at a glance who came into the room, and watch television. In the evenings, we saw the news together and then a short sequence from the comedy friends had sent him on a video for Christmas. It made us all laugh, and that pleased Alexander.

After that, it was computer time. Nothing provided him with more satisfaction than his laptop. Alexander insisted that we use the donation from England to go towards its cost. After his discharge from the clinic in Birmingham, further cheques with more money had arrived, but Alexander felt guilty about keeping them and asked me to send them back. In a moment of sheer inspiration, Ben had raced to the shops to buy Alexander a computer game that he swore his brother would love. 'See, he *does* like it and he's feeling a lot better now too,' Ben enthused. It was crucial for him to feel that he could still do *something* for his brother.

The undisputed highlight of the day, however, came when Alexander checked his incoming e-mails. Friends everywhere kept in touch, sent him little jokes, wrote him stories and kept him up to date with the latest news, and Alexander replied to each and every one of them.

Natty popped in frequently and brought with her the long essay for English that she was working on. Alexander had promised to read it through with her. He did his best. He got through the first few pages, but after that his concentration faded and he had difficulty deciphering the writing. Much to his disgust, he found he could not read his new books either and even glancing through the daily newspaper was becoming a challenge. 'I miss my books. I miss my car, too. I wish they were here, all around me,' he told us sadly. But everything was in England and there was no way we could fetch them.

One evening, we treated ourselves to cheese fondue. Alexander looked wistful and said he wanted some too. Apart from spoonfuls of ice cream and yoghurt, he had eaten practically nothing for days. I built a provisional tripod over a tea light on a tray for him to stand on his bed so he had his own fondue of sorts, then we all dunked our pieces of bread in our respective sauces and Alexander said it was the best fondue he had ever tasted.

Three times a week, we ordered an ambulance to drive Alexander to the radiotherapy department in the basement of the hospital. During the school holidays, Wolfgang accompanied him, then I took over. We always explained to the paramedics beforehand that Alexander was a terminal patient and in great pain, and suggested the best way of handling the ghastly blown-up thigh to minimize his discomfort. Most of the ambulance teams were shocked at his condition and extremely careful not to cause him more pain. But a tiny minority took no notice. They blighted our lives.

As did the radiotherapy department. The reception desk consisted of a shoulder-high wooden wall. A row of potted plants, so close that they touched, adorned the ridge and somewhere behind this fortress sat a receptionist who either steadfastly kept her eyes down or was on the phone. Sometimes we had to wait for a long time before anyone deigned to speak to us. It was true that the radiotherapy itself was painless; but lifting Alexander off the ambulance stretcher and onto the cold, hard slab under the machine in the treatment room was most certainly not. Here, too, we tried to explain Alexander's condition well in time to the staff.

Often enough, though, this was not taken seriously and I was accused of being hysterical. One assistant grabbed Alexander roughly by the tumour on his leg and, when he screamed with pain, she snapped at him and told him coldly to stop making such a fuss. The treatment times were altered at the last moment, but nobody bothered to inform us.

And there was another problem. Ambulance staff, we learnt, were responsible for delivering the patient as far as the first suitable department in the hospital, but not, of course, for carting him around within the hospital walls. That was the job of the internal transport system. Which catered for inpatients only. As he couldn't sit, Alexander could not make use of the wheelchairs available for outpatients. After radiotherapy in the basement, he sometimes needed a blood transfusion which meant some how getting to the pain control department on the ground floor.

Generally, the ambulance crew that had driven us to hospital vanished before Alexander emerged from his two-minute radiotherapy session, so he didn't even have a stretcher, let alone a bed. When I asked the lady behind the desk for a bed and offered to push him upstairs on my own, she glared at me through the screen of potted plants.

'That's not my problem. If he's that ill, he should be hospitalized,' she informed me curtly and turned her back on me. I felt very, very alone indeed.

Alexander was terrified and suffering from excruciating pain. He hated being abandoned in the middle of a room or corridor, strapped to the high, narrow ambulance stretchers. 'It feels as though it will topple over,' he told me and asked me to hold it. I could not leave him alone for a second. Weak as he was, he could not stand up for himself any more. I had to fight for him.

Only the pain control department gave us a feeling of security. Staff were always kind and understanding and did everything within their power to make life easier for us. But when it happened again that an ambulance man – although he had been warned – brutally manhandled Alexander both as he picked him from the hospital and when he brought him home, our nerves and patience were finally at an end.

I had hoped that these little outings would provide my dying son with some distraction, but more often than not they brought only mental and physical nightmares. Alexander had hoped that the radiotherapy might reduce the tumour, but the malignant cells had continued to multiply ferociously.

We exchanged looks.

'Shall I? Shall I call the hospital and say you don't want any more radiotherapy?'

He nodded in relief. We both knew that he would never again leave the room alive. When I came back from shopping later on that afternoon, a blackbird lay dead on the doorstep.

1 3

Saying Goodbye

Now we were free. Released from the terror of the ambulance transport and radiotherapy department, but also disconnected from the outside world. All the tension, the pressure of the last months, simply faded away. We had tried every avenue open to us and nothing had worked; we had no need to reproach ourselves. A sense of deep relief came over us. Being together, sharing memories, cherishing what time was left – these were the privileges we wished for most.

That our wish really did come true we owed to a unique pilot project. By now, the tumour on Alexander's thigh had reached the diameter of a middle-sized tree trunk, stretching his skin to a translucent film and reducing the rest of his body to a mere skeleton. For as long as Alexander could swallow, morphine tablets controlled the excruciating pain. But once the metastases in his lungs started to block his oesophagus, he could no longer swallow a sip of water, take a morsel of food or down even the smallest of tablets.

For most bed-ridden patients with such intense, chronic pain, this development would have meant of necessity readmission to hospital with its supply of cumbersome morphine pumps. Fortunately for us, however, our Christmas emergency had brought us into contact with the hospital's outpatient pain clinic; here we were alerted to the existence of a scheme which offered reliable, professional, all-round medical care for terminal patients with severe pain such as Alexander within their own four walls.

The pilot project consisted of the specially trained pain consultant from the hospital and an intensive care team. Dr N visited Alexander at home and, when he could no longer swallow the morphine tablets, hooked him up to a portable pump, the size of a Walkman and connected to his arm with a needle. This little machine contained a morphine cassette, the contents of which, depending on size, lasted for two to three days. Alexander's daily dosage settled down to around 1600 mg. Patients who were still mobile could return to the pain department for refills; Alexander could not. He depended on the second part of the service: an intensive care nurse specially trained in monitoring and servicing the pump, and who also acted as liaison between the pain consultant, GP and patient, and coordinated other services as appropriate.

Only about 5 per cent of all tumour patients require such intensive pain control management which can only be carried out by trained specialists, and they, we soon discovered, are few and far between. As a result, too many patients receive incompetent or – even more distressingly – no pain control at all. All too often, as we ourselves had discovered, the patient is considered to be simulating or cowardly. Sometimes, the sufferers themselves believe they have to put on a brave face and play down the extent of their pain. Conventional wisdom in both lay and medical circles continues to hold, quite mistakenly, that opioids cause addiction. Funding for research in this area is limited and much needs to be done to extend and improve training for doctors.

So we belonged to the lucky few who were able to experience an optimal care system at home. Not only did the nurse keep in constant touch with the pain consultant, but he monitored the pump, brought refills in good time, organized the other equipment and – most important of all – could reliably be reached round the clock. So we were not afraid any more. It was a wonderful feeling knowing that, at last, we had competent help at hand.

With an expert eye, the nurse saw that Alexander was uncomfortable on the mattress we had bought (with no advice and no support) and immediately ordered another one with an air pocket system. It worked with a small motor fixed to the end of the bed that pumped up the pockets in alternating rows, thus ensuring a pressure-free environment for the patient.

When he could not swallow any more, Alexander's first reaction was to refuse the offer of a drip with artificial nutrition. He didn't want any life-extending treatment, he protested. For a whole afternoon and a whole night he stuck it out. Then he gave in. The saline solution stopped him feeling thirsty, the glucose mixture made him forget his hunger, and the combination of the two greatly improved his quality of life.

Another couple of days, and breathing became arduous. Alexander struggled and gasped. The nurse ordered a home respirator and helped us set everything up. It looked like a smart, blue vacuum cleaner with an oversized umbilical cord. Because it made the most awful noise, we banned it to the basement. The cord snaked along the stairs right up to Alexander's bed.

In addition to the phone, Wolfgang installed a bell over the bed for Alexander to buzz in an emergency as he insisted on sleeping alone at night. Like this, we all felt happier in the knowledge that he could summon us quickly if need be. Altogether, we felt secure and confident.

The frailer Alexander grew, the more vital it became that he and he alone made the decisions. And for that, he needed to be told the truth. Only then could he make sensible choices.

'I'm not afraid of death,' he confided in me, 'but I am afraid of dying.' So I asked the doctor how the end would be and he explained that Alexander would slowly asphyxiate, but that he could inject a combination of tranquillizers and sedatives that would take away the fear and prevent him panicking. Taken together with the high morphine dose, however, the drugs would in all probability just bring his breathing to a gentle halt with no sensation of choking to death. I passed this information on to Alexander. He was immensely relieved. 'Then I won't need to give myself an overdose after all,' he remarked.

Peace. Quiet. Alexander dictated the day's pace. Wolfgang and Ben had breakfast in the living room before leaving for school, then I brought Alexander the utensils for washing and shaving. Performing these tasks tired him greatly, but it made him feel less of a burden on us, reinforced his independency and lent him dignity and control.

Afterwards I sat down next to the bed. Alexander's long, slender fingers reached out for mine. We talked. We discussed once more the 'why' question, and came yet again to the conclusion that probably a combination of genetic disposition, a weakened immune system as a result of his depressed state of mind and his personality structure had all played a role in the outbreak of his illness. It was nobody's fault; least of all Alexander's.

We exchanged memories of his childhood. The excitement of the annual car trip to Britain, goodnight stories sitting cosily on the sofa before bed, the day when Alexander had once set up a trap in his room to catch Father Christmas and how a bag of flour had rained down on me when I opened the door, the smell of freshly baked bread in the house, the joy of having had a brother and sister to annoy and play with, picnics in the park.

'Shall we have another picnic?' Alexander suggested on a whim. 'You can have a roll and I would like a fresh bottle of saline solution, a bit of glucose and perhaps a lick of ice cream.'

So we ate breakfast together. I watching him as he savoured the taste of ice cream on his tongue. We looked at each other and giggled madly and he said that that was nice and asked what was for dessert.

One beautiful morning he woke up and said he didn't want to die. He still had so much to do. All those books he still wanted to read, the promise of a rewarding relationship with his new girlfriend, writing a research paper on the subject of artificial intelligence, feeling the wind blowing in his face as he drove his car. No, he didn't want to say goodbye.

But the next day he changed his mind. 'Mum, would it be okay for you if I die?' he asked with a worried look on his face. I assured him that whatever he decided to do – presumably he didn't have a choice, but that was irrelevant – I would respect his decision.

'Right. Then I want to die now. I've had enough. I really did try to get well, but I couldn't manage it. I'm not just giving up.'

Of course he wasn't. And he had achieved so much in his young life. He had loved and lost and loved again. He had found many, many real friends. His dream of living in England as an Englishman had been fulfilled. He had travelled through the world. Had studied at university. Furnished a room. Owned his own car. He had – stood on his own two feet.

And seeing that the prosthesis in his left leg came from Germany and the one in his right leg from England, he was now perfectly balanced and symmetric. Not a long life, admittedly, but complete in itself. Alexander nodded in agreement.

Dying young does have its advantages, he added. He looked down at his poor broken body. A long scar ran down his left leg; a somewhat shorter one down the right leg. His thigh was so monstrously swollen we could no longer get his boxer shorts off. Both hips bore scars from the operations. The Hickmann had left an ugly mark just below the collar bone. His legs were full of metal, his lungs full of tumours.

'At least I shall never get rheumatism. Or have false teeth. Or grey hair.' He spoke with no trace of rancour.

He wanted to know how I would cope after his death.

'You will go back to teaching? How will you feel? How will you manage?'

Finding an answer was not easy. After all, I'd never had a dead son before. All I could say with certainty was that I would miss him most terribly, but that I would try and learn to live with his loss. As regards work, I promised him to either go back to teaching or to write. He approved of that and smiled contentedly.

Every day his condition deteriorated further. The pain remained under control; never quite gone, but bearable. He grew weaker and weaker. Sometimes he complained of a strange tiredness he had never experienced before. With his crutch he poked at the cushion, trying to wedge it under his leg to ease the pressure and prevent his foot from twisting. To no avail. He cried with frustration and sheer misery and would send me away to spare me the agony of watching him. Several times a day he coughed. Speaking became so arduous that he communicated in one word bulletins; phone calls with his friends were no longer possible. Even greater then was his pleasure at the daily influx of e-mails from his friends who wrote telling him how they would remember him, a gesture that brought him untold happiness and peace. In the evenings, he struggled to answer them all.

In the afternoons, Ben joined his brother in the living room. He made himself comfortable in the armchair, switched the television on, using headphones so as not to disturb Alexander, and watched one film after another. He could not bear to watch his brother dying so slowly, but he wanted to be near him nevertheless and this was his solution. From time to time he got up, held a bowl under Alexander's chin when he started to cough, wiped his face afterwards and sat down again.

More and more often Alexander told us that he felt incredibly tired and wanted to go to sleep. We understood that he would not be with us for much longer.

One evening, Ben cried bitterly and unconsolably in his bedroom. As little boys, he blurted out, he and his brother had made a solemn pact, promising each other that if one of them should ever be in trouble, the other would come to his aid. And now his brother was in trouble, terrible trouble, and Ben could see no way of keeping his pledge. He screamed his helplessness into the pillow. I sat down next to him and stroked his hair. We all wanted to help.

'You can't make him well again. But you can do the next best thing. You can stay with him and let him die in the way he wishes. That is a great help and like that you can keep your promise.'

Everybody in the family found an opportunity to be alone with Alexander. Wolfgang kept his son company late at night. Natty came to visit regularly in the afternoon and sit with her brother. She didn't need to worry about finding the right words. Alexander understood that his brother and sister were at his side, that was the important point.

Despite the respirator, Alexander gasped for air. We could have done with a fan. Ben scoured the whole of town but none of the shops stocked this summer item in the middle of winter and he returned empty-handed.

Outside it was icy cold. At night, the thermometer sank to well below minus 10 degrees. Whenever Alexander thought he was suffocating — and he thought that very often — we had to open the balcony door, not just a crack, but wide open. Subjectively, he imagined he could breathe again and after a few minutes would allow us — we were frozen to the core — to shut the door again.

After some discussion with our GP, the pain consultant suggested puncturing Alexander's lung. If any fluid had collected there, it could then be drained off and that might ease his breathing problems. With a local anaesthetic, the whole thing would be quite painless. Alexander thought it over and gave his consent.

As we were alone at home, I had to act as assistant. Three times the long needle vanished inside Alexander's chest. Three times the syringe turned red.

'Alexander, it's no good,' Dr N told him gently. 'There is no fluid in there. It's all full of metastases.'

Alexander nodded wearily. We couldn't even make that more comfortable for him. I cried with helpless anger.

It was time for the tranquillizers and sedatives. We knew that each injection could be the last. We watched beads of sweat form on his brow as the nurse carefully measured out the correct amount in the evening and slowly injected it. Alexander was frightened of sleeping alone now. We moved mattresses into the living room. After that first dose, he seemed to have passed the night peacefully; his breathing came regularly. But when he woke up in the morning, he cursed to find himself still alive. All night long, unknown to us, he had been suffering from nightmares and hallucinations.

I could no longer leave him alone for a second. Once I had just wanted to go to the toilet quickly, but I only got as far as the kitchen when Alexander cried out: 'Mum! Come! Leg burst! Help!' I ran back. The black spiral cord from the remote control was lying across his leg and Alexander had thought his main artery had broken through the skin. Wolfgang and Ben came home at lunchtimes and I had cooked nothing to eat.

Sometimes Alexander was confused, but always realized immediately that he had been talking nonsense. Most of the time he lay without moving in bed, his eyes half-closed and rolled upwards. The crutch lay next to him in bed. He didn't use it any more. One day I removed it and he didn't notice. But he wasn't unconscious and, when I told him what I was doing, he nodded and understood every word.

Towards the evening, the soporific effect of the medication began to wear off and he could talk a little to us. I asked him what he was thinking of. He didn't really know, he said, but now that we had changed the medicine, the thoughts were of an agreeable nature.

'What's the difference between the euro and the ecu? I can't remember and I'd really like to know,' he asked me suddenly. That was no confused state of mind. That was Alexander.

Did he think that death was near? Again, he couldn't say for sure. I asked him if he would like to hear about my mother's last hours and he said, yes, he would. So I told him again how his grandmother had slipped into unconsciousness and then died peacefully early in the morning. Why? Because of the biological rhythm. That's how it is with many people. Probably he too would die before sunrise. He nodded thoughtfully. I promised to stay with him always, even if he lost consciousness. Unless, of course, he would rather be alone.

'No. Die with you.'

And I showed him the simple white candle that we would light for him after his death, told him he would stay with us in the living room for quite a while afterwards. He smiled and said that it all sounded very nice.

The following morning, he woke up feeling much better. So much better that we dared wash his sticky hair and change his clothes. At teatime, Alexander announced he was hungry! To our utter amazement and delight, we watched as he actually managed to swallow a sliver of flat noodle! Then he switched on the laptop and his face lit up. 'Wow! Fourteen e-mails!' It was a wonderful day. Alexander was glad to be alive. I hoped there would be more days like that.

But the next morning things started going downhill again. It was increasingly difficult for us to understand what Alexander was saying to us. On 22 January, the postman delivered two parcels. One was from his girlfriend. I read the accompanying letter out loud to him. He listened with shut eyes. When I'd finished, a smile flickered over his face.

The other packet had been sent by a friend of his and contained a book. A quick glance at the jacket cover revealed it was by Arthur C. Clarke. Alexander had already read it. What a relief. He was too tired to listen to that letter as well, so I put both it and the book in his drawer, meaning to read it to him later.

Three times that day, Alexander knocked over his full urine bottle. His co-ordination was failing dismally. He pushed the wrong button on his remote control and the whole bed drifted slowly upwards towards the ceiling; he didn't seem to have noticed.

'What on earth are you doing?' I asked him.

'Going up to the angels,' he joked and grinned.

To all intents and purposes he appeared to be asleep, but in fact he was wide awake. Throughout the day, I stroked him, told him I loved him and he whispered back that he loved us all too and he smiled.

The nurse persuaded him that the time for a urinary catheter had come and fitted him out accordingly. His boxer shorts were cutting into his flesh – we would have had to cut them open in order to take them off. Alexander said that could wait until the next day.

There was a ring at the doorbell. A colleague of mine had cooked us a complete dinner and brought it over, just like that. What a godsend! And more than welcome as we had a visitor, Uli, a family friend of ours, and he was famished after driving to us after a long day's work as a doctor in a hospital in Munich. Alexander was pleased to see him again.

'Hungry. Ice cream,' he mumbled. We brought him a scoop of ice cream. He tried to navigate the spoon to his mouth, and missed.

'Dad. Feed me,' he said.

Dr N dropped in. He should have changed the needle in his patient's arm, but Alexander hated the pricking. The doctor left things as they were. 'Thank you,' Alexander said.

The nurse came and listened to the way Alexander was breathing in and out. He thought it wouldn't take much longer.

We rang Natty and asked her to come straight away and spend the night with us. She came. Now all five of us were reunited under one roof.

Alexander repeated how tired he was. He wanted to sleep. The others went upstairs and I prepared to sleep with him in the living room.

'Quick. Mum. So ti-red.'

But no sooner had I turned off the light than he started fumbling around for the switch on his lamp.

'What's the matter?'

'Pissed in bed. Bad,' he whispered.

That couldn't be – he had the catheter now. I pulled back the bed-clothes to investigate. The needle in his arm had slipped and blood was oozing out and dripping onto his shorts. He was greatly relieved to hear that he hadn't wetted the bed. What a bit of luck that we had a doctor in the house. I fetched Uli to sort everything out.

'Don't prick. Please.'

Alexander was terrified, but Uli did a marvellous job of sliding the old needle back into position without having to prick.

Back to bed. Several times Alexander gasped 'door' and I leapt up and flung open the balcony door and the icy-cold air that he couldn't breathe wafted into the room. I was frozen to the bone. But Alexander's skin was warm.

At some point in the night, Wolfgang joined me and for a while took over being doorman. I dozed. In the dark, I was half aware of Alexander's laborious breathing and Wolfgang asking him whether he wished to be given the injection the nurse had left for us and Alexander saying, yes. Then Wolfgang shook me fully awake. 'He's going,' he told me.

We called the others down and gathered round the bed. Uli checked Alexander's pulse. It was still flickering – just. And then, very quietly and very peacefully, it stopped. It was 6.30 in the morning.

We turned all the machines off, lit the candle and sat round him, holding his hands and stroking his lovely blond hair until the sun rose in the east on that freezing but sunny 23 January.

The two men walked down to the baker's to buy rolls. When they came back, we all sat down together at the dining table in the living room and drank coffee and had a bite of breakfast and felt very close to Alexander.

Not until late afternoon did we call the undertakers. The men pulled him out of his bed, dressed him in a white silk shirt he would have hated, screwed up his blood-red T-shirt and dropped it behind the sofa and lay our son and brother in a coffin on our living room rug. Then they trooped out for a smoke in the hallway. We gave Alexander a red rose and a coin for good luck and I kissed his cold forehead before they closed the lid and took him away. He was 22 years old.

Once the rental company had collected the bed, and the nurse packed up all the drips and stands and bottles and bandages, the room echoed emptily. Strange, then, when the now quiet house filled up a few days later with visitors for the funeral.

Every room had an occupant, even the living room. In the hall at the cemetery, Alexander's flower-covered coffin stood at the front, flanked on each side by two beautiful bouquets of flowers sent by the University of Warwick and the Department of Computer Science. Alexander's friends found the words. One described the time spent together in the clinic in Hamburg, Philipp the years at grammar school, another – in English – his time at university in England, and Wolfgang reminded us of our son's love of books and literature, his deep-seated relationship to both England and Germany, his courage in the face of illness and his peaceful death. We buried him on the hill-top cemetery, facing north, under a blue Portuguese stone, a rose engraved over his name and the words 'dearly loved' under it.

It was so cold that we brought the bouquets home, adding them to the others in the living room. A magnificent display. They warmed us for days with their spring colours until they too began to fade, wilted and died.

A few weeks later, Wolfgang, Natty and Ben flew to England to attend a memorial service for Alexander held at the university. The hall was overflowing and Alexander's Director of Studies held a speech. After everyone had selected a book from Alexander's collection to remember him by, we donated his library to the university. His beloved car they brought back home. Friends planted trees for Alexander at the university, in a commemorative woodland just outside Coventry, and in Lincoln, in the cemetery near his favourite bookshop 'Reader's Rest'.

I had forgotten all about the book. I found it and the unread letter still in the drawer while I was tidying up. I skimmed through the lines. Something about going to his house, asking him for a favour and him saying of course he would do it. Nothing of any importance, it seemed. I picked up the book – Rendezvous with Rama – and on some impulse, opened it. On the inside page I noticed something red and hand-written. I started to read.

'To Alex, with best wishes Arthur C. Clarke'. Signed, fourth January.

1 4

Bridges

They blew up the little footbridge over the motorway. A short detonation in the early hours of the morning and the connecting element between home and hospital was destroyed, leaving behind a yawning gap, a deep hole.

Gaps appeared all over the place. In the living room, I missed the bed I used to sit next to. I had no cause to go to the hospital any more and there were no nurses or doctors to let into the house. Only the brown envelopes with bills that continued to plop into the letter box every morning provided a certain continuity.

Alexander's bed left a physical void too in the corner that we filled with a strong, young cheese plant. Within a short time, it had produced a ladder of shiny fresh leaves right up to the ceiling. For a long time I found it difficult to move away from this place; I could still hear the machines humming, still waited with bated breath for him to call me, for his fingers to curl round mine. Sitting there made me feel connected with him; going away felt like abandoning him.

Gaps, too, in my memory. I have only hazy recollections of the events of the following weeks. In our minds, we had known that our child would die, but the actual event nevertheless led to a perfectly normal shock reaction – we still had to understand with our hearts. When, a mere week after the funeral, somebody cheerfully volunteered the opinion that I must certainly have 'got over it by now', I burst into tears.

After the long years of unbroken strain, faultlines, cavities, gaps became apparent everywhere. With no pressing reason to get up in the morning, I soon realized just how physically exhausted I really was. My concentration waned, my appetite swung wildly between wanting to eat nothing at all or craving for comfort foods. And sounds. Even the most beautiful rendering of a symphony hurt my ears and seemed to tie a rope tightly around my chest until I could hardly breathe. I longed for peace and silence.

Yet at the same time, some of the holes started filling up. Imperceptibly and slowly at first, but gradually gaining ground. The many letters of condolence comforted me greatly. The rector of Warwick University wrote personally, as did the senior consultant of the Royal Orthopaedic Hospital in Birmingham, the staff on the ward and the social worker who – as promised – offered a lifeline of support by phone or letter over the following years.

One sunny morning in February, a letter arrived from England. It was from the wife of the patient in the Royal Orthopaedic Hospital in Birmingham whom Alexander had been able to help with his cheque. Also in the envelope, I found a photo of a pretty little baby. She and her husband had become the proud parents of a baby boy three weeks after Alexander's death, she wrote, and in memory of our son had named their first-born Alexander. I was so very touched and extremely proud too.

The summer term with its commitments started. But without me. I just did not feel up to teaching classes. Everything lay shattered and broken around me, infinite devastation as far as I could see. But amongst the ruins, I discovered a handful of word fragments and found I could stick them together to form chains. Some of them fell apart again immediately, but others held and they constituted the first make-shift footbridge. I began to write small, provisional bridges (articles for the regional newspaper), which then grew into air bridges (articles for publications abroad) and eventually evolved into a load-carrying suspension bridge – this book.

Natty and Ben were worse off as they had no choice. Both of them had to juggle their grief with revision, both of them struggled with crucial exams at school, Natty had to finish her long essay. Yet she managed admirably, doggedly withstanding the pressure of daily school routine, sitting her leaving examinations in May and gaining such an excellent result that nothing stood between her and a place at university.

A year later and Ben followed in his siblings' footsteps. For him too, it meant navigating mourning, phases of depression, endless tests and the stress of examinations. But he achieved an equally good result before he then embarked on his year's civilian service in another hospital in our town.

And there was a new bridge linking us to England. Coventry is the birthplace of 'The Compassionate Friends', a now international self-help organization for parents who have suffered the loss of a child of any age and from any cause. It offers a worldwide network of support, warmth and friendship. A well-equipped postal library, quarterly newsletter with contributions on various subjects by the bereaved parents themselves, a series of practical leaflets, e-mail contacts, chatrooms, a telephone hotline and an annual national gathering are available to parents, siblings, grandparents and friends of the deceased child, no matter where they live in the world.

Being together with other people who have endured similar experiences can be a healing process. Being in the shelter of a group that understands shored up my confidence, especially when the bridges to the non-bereaved frequently came crashing down.

We were often on the receiving end of such well-meant advice as 'life goes on' or 'everyone has his cross to bear'. Or the conversation exhausted itself in admonitions: 'You should', 'You mustn't', or 'You must'. Many people said nothing; avoided us, crossed to the other side of the road. That did not help us at all. On the contrary. It left us facing a wall of silence. Because they did not take our fears, anger and sorrow seriously but tried instead to repress them, they effectively blocked a constructive conversation right from the very beginning.

The best support came from those who simply listened to us, let us talk, allowed us to express our grief even if it meant that we cried, who shared their memories of Alexander with us, lit candles for him on his birthday and anniversary or sent cards and continue to do so. They are the ones who help us build bridges from the past to the future.

Anyone who thought about the siblings also did us a great service. People often asked how old my other children were, but when they heard the numbers 20 and 18, they breathed a sigh of relief and said, oh well, then they are *adults,* as though that somehow eliminated the need for support and empathy. And it is infinitely easier to drum up an image of a physical illness than a mental one. But the effects of both are horrific.

Prompted perhaps by her brother's death from cancer, Natty's condition subsequently deteriorated further. Her addiction problems reached a new negative peak and resulted in her dropping out of university. But there is a glimmer of hope: she is undergoing a long-term therapy in a drug clinic and looking forward to standing on her own two feet, just like her two brothers.

Hospital and home are separated no longer; they have grown together. Where once the little footbridge carried us over the motorway chasm, a metre-long tunnel now contains the roar of traffic. A thick roof of white concrete has filled in the gap, like resin on a wound. The edges are still jagged, cannot yet be walked on, but soon plants will be growing on the sturdy new surface, reuniting the once separated sides.

Useful Organizations

The British and Irish Chapter of the International Association for the Study of Pain
9 Bedford Square
London WC1B 3RE
painsoc@compuserve.com

Douglas House Hospice (A respite for young people)
110 St. Mary's Road
Oxford OX4 1QD
douglashouse@ukonline.co.uk

CLIC – Cancer and Leukaemia in Children
Abbeywood Business Park
Filton
Bristol BS34 7JU
Tel: 0117 311 2600
www.clic.org.uk

The Compassionate Friends
National Office
53 North Street
Bristol BS3 1EN
info@tcf.org.uk
www.tcf.org.uk
Tel: 01179 665 202

Cruse Bereavement Care
126 Sheen Road
Richmond TW9 1UR
Tel: 020 8939 9530

Teenage Cancer Trust
38 Warren Street
London
W1T 6AE
www.teencancer.org/z/frames2.html
Tel: 020 7837 1000

Recommended Reading

Grinyer, A. (2002) *Cancer in Young Adults: Through Parents' Eyes.* Maidenhead: Open University Press.

Webster Blank, J. (1998) *The Death of an Adult Child: A Book for and About Bereaved parents.* New York: Baywood Publishing Company, Inc.